A BACKPACKING ADVENTURE ACROSS THE USA AND THROUGH CENTRAL AMERICA

Sequel to Wanderlust. A life driven by the desire for global travel

Paul Holt

ISBN-9798710590300

Cover design by: Art Painter
Library of Congress Control Number: 2018675309
Printed in the United States of America

For Chris Lewis.
Taken from us far too soon, but not forgotten.

CONTENTS

Title Page

Copyright

Dedication

Introduction. 1

The USA and Mexico. 3

Guatemala and El Salvador. 31

Honduras and Nicaragua. 51

Costa Rica and Panamá. 92

INTRODUCTION.

The kindle book cover photo of Wanderlust, the girl beach vendor exhibiting her goods for sale, one of mine and Ally's favourite pictures, taken in India in 1992, is the image you need to find for my facebook page displaying all the photographs related to both books. Search Paul Holt, a very common name, and scroll down until you find that portrait, shown here. Send me a friend request, and I will accept it, so you can view the snapshots I took along the way. It will enhance the story somewhat if you can see the illustrations.

I highly recommend that you read Wanderlust. A life driven by the desire for global travel. It gives you the backstory of how I think I took to globetrotting. It was my first attempt at writing, so it's a bit clumsy, and probably too honest, but I had determined on a warts and all account of my beginnings of a life as a traveller. I was no angel, but I worked things out along the way, like most people do I guess. You can take a peek inside before you buy it, to see the contents, which are the countries I visited, and travelled through in my early days as a wanderer. The introduction and the first major backpacking trip when me and Ally explored India and some of the far east. All the short trips through the 90s and into the noughties. The second half of Wanderlust is about my first year long trip to Australia, New Zealand, South East Asia, Sri Lanka and The Maldives, before embarking on a fantastic six month adventure through sub Saharan Africa. It ends with me returning home after fourteen months on the road in about March 2004, and this second book, A backpacking adventure across the USA and through Central America, picks up from the end of my first book. Thank you so much for taking the trouble to read it; I hope you enjoy it.

THE USA AND MEXICO.

It was nice to be back for a while, though I was once again, disappointed but not particularly surprised, that very few people showed much interest in my travels. I guess that you have to want to travel yourself to enjoy listening to other people's tales. It irked me mildly when people told me I was fortunate to live the life that I had created for myself, there was not a single element of luck involved, I had engineered this life over the past ten years. I had become the creator of my own destiny. I had a good catch up with most of my friends and family, a smattering of enjoyable photo sessions for the few who were fascinated, and generally settled back into Chippenham culture. Gina had re met a childhood sweetheart, and was living with him, so I had the house to myself. Marc told me one night when he came round to play chess, that he had come in one day to use the toilet, he had a key, and the place was a tip. That was before Gina came back from Australia, when her previous boyfriend had been looking after the property, obviously not very well, having parties most weekends it seemed. I didn't care really, she had obviously made it ship shape again.

So, I might as well get a job instead of spending the money I've got, and I still have a couple more buyout payments to be debited into my account, so the next trip was already secured money wise, and was very keen now to learn Spanish and explore Central America. I got employment with a local crash barrier maintenance firm, and worked with a guy called Chris. We would drive to a depot on the M11, which was the northern part of the M25. Our section of the M25 motorway was the north east quarter, so after picking up our work schedule, the traffic management would put on the lane closures, and we would drive the van and lorry in to replace beams and posts that had been hit by vehicles. It could only be done during the early morning hours, as the M25 is so busy, even at night the trucks coming from the ports were continuous; a far cry from the peacefulness of travel in Africa, and I often felt overwhelmed by the hecticness of the job. But the money was very good, and I really enjoyed working with Chris.

He had travelled a lot himself before settling down, including an African trip, so we had a variety of common ground. I knew him from around the pubs, he was a bit younger than me, but very laid back, and was nearly always in a happy mood. We usually toked on the return journey, and one night, I was driving back, and it felt like I was playing a game on a console, so I pulled into Reading services and let him drive the rest of the way. He had been doing the job most of his adult life, so was used to the seemingly endless hours behind the wheel, and was one of the best drivers I ever knew. So, I started to drive there through the evening, and he would do the stint back home. I quite often expressed my concern for the franticness of the work, but Chris was very reassuring and said I couldn't leave as he liked having me as his labourer.

One night, we were just finishing up tensioning the beam that we had replaced. Suddenly, an Indian chap was with us asking for directions! Chris fucked him off back to his car, parked on the hard shoulder, and demanded that he get on his way, which he did. When he returned to me, he said, "For a minute there, I thought you'd ordered a takeaway."

Another night we were heading along the M4, listening to some music, nicely chilled from the joint we'd shared. It was maybe 3am, the road was virtually unoccupied, and we were cruising at over 100mph. Gotta say, them vans were perfectly designed for that type of work, low centre of gravity and extra wide tyres for superb grip on the asphalt. We were coming past one of the Reading junctions, and I caught a flash of blue light in the passenger wing mirror, and said to Chris, "police, I think." He replied that he had clocked them, but didn't even ease off the gas a millimetre. The cop car was overtaking us on the slip road, so was doing more than a ton, and joined the motorway in front of us, blues and twos flashing, as it eased ahead of us. Trippy as fuck. As we were doing 100 plus, it took awhile for the police car to disappear from view. Chris barely blinked, it was a totally normal situation for him.

The night before I jacked the job in, a serious incident took place that rattled me beyond my ability to withstand the manic nature of the livelihood. We had a two lane closure as the run of the barrier to be replaced was fairly long. So, there was only one live lane and the traffic was heavy even at 1am. The taper from three lanes to one lane is about a mile and plenty of signage on approach. However, someone had decided, driving a smallish car, to try and get in front of a line of trucks. The cone shaped bollards that protect any work force have big rubber feet, and are designed to stop vehicles plowing into the roadworks. A sudden loud noise reached us, crashing and smashing sounds, and we looked down the highway to see a car landing on its roof inside the works. Chris immediately started running down to it, a couple hundred metres away, and I instinctively started after him. I was thinking that I was now going to see a mashed up dead body inside the car, and really wasn't looking forward to that one little bit; as I've said before, I'm squeamish about such things. When Chris got there, the traffic was now fully stopped and backing up rapidly, he discovered the car empty of human presence! He seemed confused. Just then, I saw a guy a little way away, talking on a mobile phone! I approached him, to ask what he was doing there? He put his hand up to me indicating that he was in the middle of a conversation! I heard him explaining to someone that he would be late because he had broken down! He was the driver of the car now upside down and the top half flattened somewhat! We got details of the front truck driver in case a witness was needed, then got the traffic moving again. Shortly afterwards, the police arrived and we went back to finish the task in hand. Chris seemed completely unflustered by the whole occurrence, saying it was quite a regular event! But I was shaken, and when I got home, I sat and drank a couple of beers and decided to quit the next day. Chris was disappointed, but understood, such was his lovely nature.

I got chatting to Tony in the pub over the weekend, and they were on a job in Henley on Thames, replumbing an old brewery building being converted to a hotel. He said they could do with a labourer, and would speak to his boss about employing me. So started my new career as a plumber's mate, working with Tony and Simo, putting up brackets to hold pipe to begin with. A much more relaxed workplace, and I progressed to do quite a lot of pipework, taught how to solder and many other tasks. My tea making skills have always stood me in good stead over the years, I can knock up a good brew. We were staying in a caravan on a park near the site, and earning enough to eat out most evenings and have a round of drinks, plus lots of playing pool. I quite liked the banter around a building site, you hear a lot of swearing and you tend to swear a lot yourself, just goes with the territory. Everyone else who worked there was sound, and health and safety in the UK was strict enough that you are never expected to do anything dangerous. In fact, it became too over the top in the succeeding years, and everyone was forced to do courses which you had to pay for, to be allowed on a site; and renew them every five years! Another little money making racket.

Ally wanted to take the kids to Zante for a week. She had Kyle who was still a toddler of three, and Blake who was about nine or ten, a foster son that she was taking care of. She wasn't with Kyle's father anymore, so asked me if I would come along to help her out, and, of course, enjoy a little break. It wasn't expensive, so I booked a weeks' holiday, and we flew out when the Euros were on and checked into a sweet little apartment. Turned out that my sister Tina, brother in law, Julian and my two nieces, Stevie and Shannon were there also during the same time, so we caught up a couple of evenings when England were playing. I hired a quad bike and took the kids on rides; Blake was dying to ride it, so I let him have a go up and down the track by the accommodation. He was fine, but, one time when he was trying to turn around, he ended up in the farmer's field, crushing the marrows, so I had to run up and help him, before the farmer spotted him.

One extraordinary incident was, we were heading to the beach one evening with Kyle in his buggy, to go and eat at a restaurant there. On the way, a street dog loped past, stopping to have a little sniff of Kyle, who gave it a pat on the head, then it continued on its way. We had our meal, then the kids wanted to paddle, so we sat chatting and drinking, while they played in the shallows. Blake was instructed to look out for his brother and, of course we were keeping an eye on them also. A minute passed since we last looked over, and Kyle was gone! We raced down to ask Blake where he was? He didn't know! I scanned the water, not seeing anything, and started to jog along the shoreline in one direction, Ally and Blake in the other. I asked some people, and others got involved in the search. Just then, the same dog from earlier, came up to me barking, and started back the way it had appeared from! Checking over its shoulder to make sure I was following. I wasn't sure what was going on, it all seemed very surreal, but was clutching at straws by then, and jogged after the dog. Then I saw Kyle, and ran to pick him up, bewildered by how far away he'd got to in the short space of time. He didn't supply us with answers unfortunately, but we were just mightily glad to have him back, it could have been disastrous. The dog showing me his location was utterly bizarre, and I understood better that animals must have an intelligence that wasn't really credited to them.

The job was alright, it suited me, there was no stress involved, I just had to work through the tasks that were allocated to me: Tony or Simo helped me when something was beyond my capabilities. The most shocking thing in my whole life happened one morning. Ally phoned me and told me to sit down, then proceeded to inform me that Chris had been killed the night before at work. It was a terrible time, and I returned to Chippenham that evening to mourn him with the rest of the townspeople. The details were very distressing to hear, and the guy who was with him, Chris had saved his life at the expense of his own, had to undertake counselling. The funeral took place and the church was full, many more people outside in the churchyard and even out of the gates. Must have been thousands of grieving folk there, many tears were shed, a testament to Chris's popularity.

Nothing remains quite the same after such a traumatic event. He was talked about a lot, keeping the memory of him alive. Chippenham had a sombre ambiance for years. I went back to work and was by now starting to think about the winter trip, which was already decided would be Central America, and I obtained a second hand copy of the Lonely planet for that region. About mid September, 2004, I bought a return flight to New York for October 10th, the leg home booked for early May 2005. An old friend, Rob, was living and working in New Mexico, so I would be visiting him before heading south to the border, pretty much the only plan I made. Gina had informed me that she now wanted to sell her half of the house as she would be getting married to John and living there permanently. I persuaded her to put it off until next year, and we organised renting it out for six months, hoping that the income would change her mind. To buy her out again would now cost me 60 grand, 10 more than the original mortgage that I had.

I was 40 at the end of September, and a surprise party was held for me. Steve and Maike came, and it ended up being a raucous, drink and drug fuelled bender. Early on, there was a tap on my shoulder as I was talking to someone, and I turned to see a police woman! I groaned, understanding immediately what was coming, she was the stripper that a few of my 'friends' had organised. How embarrassing, in front of my older and younger family members. I really wished that they hadn't done that, but I went through the motions, not wanting to be a killjoy either.

A few news stories that were of interest during 2004 and into 2005, were that there was the largest expansion of NATO, with seven extra European countries joining. The Hamas leader was killed in The Gaza strip. Ten more countries joined The European Union. Portugal hosted the Euros, which was won by Greece when we were there, a massive party got underway. The US coalition transferred sovereignty to an Iraqi interim government, and the preliminary hearings of Saddam Hussein's trial began. The Cassini space probe arrived at Saturn. The 2004 Olympic games were hosted by Athens in Greece. Two aircraft exploded over Russia, and Chechen suicide bombers were blamed. There was suicide bombings in Taba, Egypt. George W Bush got reelected as US president. 200,000 people lost their lives after a massive earthquake off the coast of Sumatra caused an Indian ocean wide tsunami. North Korea announced that it had nukes. Hariri, the Lebanese prime minister, was assassinated in Beirut. YouTube was launched. The Kyoto protocol came into effect, and another earthquake in North Sumatra. Pope John Paul 2nd died and Benedict the 16th took over. Syria withdrew from Lebanon. And the superjumbo jet Airbus A380 made its maiden flight.

Until I was 45, you could buy cheap backpacker travel insurance, for about £150 for six months, so I had purchased that before I left. I drove Dad's car to Heathrow, with Mum and Dad as passengers, he would obviously be driving back. It was always a bit heart rending saying goodbye to Mum, as she looked so sad, but managed not to blubber as we parted company. Someone had told me you should always ask for a free upgrade, and occasionally, you got lucky. My very first time trying that, I got an affirmative, and flew in economy plus, considerably more comfortable, so slept well on that transAtlantic crossing. The many hours time difference meant that we landed the same day, most likely late afternoon. I hadn't thought through a story to tell immigration, and was questioned, so told the guy what I was intending. Busing to New Mexico, then heading down into Central America, and travelling all the way to Panama. He gave me a quizzical look, then a big smile and said, "man, that sounds great. You have a good trip now." I'm assuming that I had secured my visa waiver in advance. The arrival airport was Newark, I collected my bag and, leaving the airport, there were some phones and numbers for hotels. I spoke to a few of them, all expensive, so I went out to ask a taxi driver, who recommended Elizabeth as a base, and took me to a motel there that was $50 for a decent room. The billboard had advertised movies, so I flicked the tv on and surfed the channels, coming across a porn station. So that was what 'movies' meant on a motel sign! After a shower, I went out to find beer and food. No beer in the shops, and I ended up with a tin of macaroni and minced beef, and ate it using pork rinds as a spoon. Then read for a while and slept early.

I was trying to give up smoking, for a while at least, and had brought with me a nicotine nasal spray. After using it, I sneezed about 25 or 30 times, not great, don't think I'm gonna stick with that. I paid another night, then walked to the train station, seeing Sam's diner en route and stopped for a cheap very good breakfast, but struggled to get black tea. I ended up with some flavoured infusion, that didn't give me my caffeine fix. I tried some coffee, but couldn't drink it, I have no idea why I don't like coffee? The train takes you into the heart of Manhattan at Pennsylvania station or just simply Penn. It turned out that it was Columbus day, so a bank holiday and lots of people about. I spent the day walking the streets, marvelling at the high rise, steam actually does come from the manhole covers like in the movies, and people say God damn it and holy shit. I wandered through Greenwich village with all the cafes from every country on Earth it seemed. Made my way to Ground Zero and read about what was intended to be done with the site. Then to the ferry terminal for The Statue of Liberty, but there was a massive queue, so I sat on a bench eating a fruit cake that Maike had bought me for my birthday, gazing at the famous monument. Back to The Empire State Building, paying $12 to go to the top, the feeling of vertigo had my testicles retreating inside of me and tingling with alarm. The Skyride, virtual tour over NYC, was great fun, very well done.

At the magnificent Grand Central station, I tried to find out about trains to Taos, New Mexico, where Rob lived, but it was all a bit vague, and no one seemed particularly interested in selling me a ticket. At the Greyhound bus depot, I was greeted very warmly by a John Candy lookalike. So enthusiastic when I told him where I wanted to go, and he got on his computer and routed me there, with a stopover in St Louis and Denver. He talked the whole time, and had me very excited about the journey, and it wasn't even terribly expensive either. After I'd paid, and he'd printed the tickets, he said, "you have a good day now, and thank you for your custom." He really got me stoked up for the two day, two night crossing of the USA. I returned to Elizabeth and stopped for a steak feed and a couple of beers, and managed to buy a couple of smokes off someone, not wanting to buy a whole packet. I got a phone card and phoned Mum, Ally, then Rob, to tell him I was on my way.

The alarm clock went off at 4am, I was mostly packed up, so after ablutions, I checked out and got a taxi to the train station. Sam's was open, so got a small breakfast, then on the train to Penn and walked to the Greyhound terminal. There was a short delay, but then we were on our way, and heading back through Newark, and out into some countryside, with glorious autumn colours on the expanse of forest. Trenton and onwards to Philadelphia, in the state of Pennsylvania, which appeared to be a small clean city. At King of Prussia, a strange name for a town, there was quite a thorough security check, by armed and stern looking cops. Vast swathes of woodland or forest made magnificent by the array of shades of yellows, oranges, reds, purples and browns, gave me a lot of satisfaction, so pleasing to the eye. In Harrisburg, my companion got down, and the next one to sit by me was a rather large gentleman with bad breath, who insisted on talking a lot, which was very whiffy. A food stop in Carlisle, then blankets of trees in all their splendour, for tens of miles at a time; maybe The USA is environmentally sound after all? At Pittsburgh station, I bought a cigarette for 25 cents, and it was blissful. Then on route 70, dark by now, to Columbus in Ohio, Indianapolis, Indiana, Effingham, Illinois, and finally to St Louis, Missouri at 7.30am the following morning. I mostly slept, which was good.

I helped a girl with her plentiful baggage, the taxi drivers trying to tout for my business, but I felt like walking. The hotels were expensive, but a lady at the Holiday inn, told me of the Econo lodge, so I went there and got a room for $63. Into town, and a decent breakfast again at a diner, struggling with tea, so I went to a shop and found some black tea bags. You could use the internet for free at libraries, so I sent a few mails, and scanned the news. A guy who I got chatting to, told me he was the great grandson of Winston Churchill? Another guy said he used to be a policeman in Alaska, he had cigarettes, so I bought one off him, 25 cents seemed to be acceptable. Everybody I talked to said, "oh, you're from Australia." The Mississippi river runs through St Louis, so I wandered to a bridge and stood watching that other great snaking waterway for a while. There was a kettle in the room, so I got some milk and made tea at the digs. Relaxed for a few hours, reading and channel surfing, then a shave and shower. A Chinese feed, and a bar for a couple, before going back to try and sleep a bit. It was 11.45pm when I woke up, so dozed a bit longer, then got a lift from Omar back to the station. Bought a sarnie, checked in, and shortly on our way again.

Slept until we pulled into Kansas city terminal, at 6.45am. Got some hot water to put in a polystyrene cup with a tea bag, and a hot dog for breaky. A lady was talking to herself, quite animatedly! We are now on the Great plains of central USA, lots of very flat land, which is now mainly farms, the wheat belt, but think it has been harvested. Livestock, cattle, including Ankole, or Big horn. Big metal constructions everywhere, that looked like giant praying mantises, the heads bobbing up and down, which turned out to be oil pumps, a lot of crude in the ground apparently. We stopped in Topeka, then for lunch in Salina, had a subway, and bought another stick to suck on, getting a nicotine fix. The featureless landscape seemed endless, totally flat for hundreds of miles. Read quite a lot, and a guy was telling me that there are Air force bases built into the mountains. In Colby, as the sun was setting, you start to get glimpses of the Rocky mountains, getting interesting scenery just as night is falling. Bit more shut eye, nothing to look at now, and arrived in Denver after 8pm, where we had a three hour stopover. I got chatting to a girl from Montana, and bought another fag. The next and final leg got underway before midnight, and slept mostly until sunup as we pulled into Taos.

I knew Rob was quite a heavy smoker, so that was the end of my little smoking detox. I bought a packet from the shop and waited for Rob to turn up. A young guy called Jason approached me asking how I was getting to town, and I said I would ask Rob when he got here if he would give him a lift. A few minutes later, Rob showed up in an old Ford pick up truck. And of course it was alright to give Jason a lift. He got in the middle and I sat by the passenger window, and we started chatting as he began to head back to town. It was great to see him again, and we exchanged some info about people we knew back home; he'd heard about Chris's tragic death. He'd been there several years and was now an illegal alien. He looked past Jason, and asked me if I had any fags? Jason visibly tensed up. Rob burst out laughing, and quickly explained that fags was a slang name for cigarettes in the UK. Jason couldn't get his fags out quick enough, he was so relieved, that he wasn't suddenly in the midst of two raging faggots.

We dropped him off in town, then to Rob's place a little way out, set alone on a decent sized plot of land. Rob had to go to work, so I made tea, and finished up some spaghetti bolognese that he said I could have. I grabbed another two to three hours of slumber, then took a walk into the central plaza. Nice place, bit touristy, but charming and out of season now, in between the summer and ski season. Bought the latest National Geographic magazine, and got some shopping before heading back. It's a very picturesque location, the Sangre de Cristo mountains surround the settlement of only a few thousand people and sits at an elevation of a little over 2000 metres. Turned out that there are two houses joined together, and I met Rob's neighbour, Jennifer, and had a chat with her. I read four corners, a book on the shelf, as Rob had told me we were going to be doing a road trip. I had a nice relaxing bath, and Rob got back about 5pm, cracking the top off the first coldie of the day, and continuing to catch up. When I had called from the UK to check whether I was welcome to come visit, I had asked if there was anything I could bring with me that he was missing? Rob said to bring him some Branston pickle, so I gave him the two big jars that had survived the journey, and I think they were devoured fairly quickly. We went to his local, it was Friday night, so he could drink as he wasn't going to work tomorrow. Ended up playing shuffleboard, meeting lots of his friends and got pissed up.

A good lie in, bit hungover, and when Rob got up, we went for breakfast at a local cafe, meeting Neil, a guy who Rob worked with. Rob and Jenny were going to a wedding, so a friend called Diana came to collect me and babysit me for the afternoon.

We immediately fell into a rapport, her being very easy to converse with, an environmentalist, so had a huge amount of talking points. She showed me her house, which she'd done up herself, and I met her dogs. We went with the dogs to The Rio Grande gorge bridge and hiked along for quite a while, before turning back. The scenery was gorgeous, and the conversation never let up, and she asked if I could help her out a couple days next week. Rob had told me that we were setting off on our road trip Friday, so I jumped at the chance for something to do for a day or two. We went to see some off grid houses where she knew one of the owners, completely self sufficient, solar panels and wind turbines, bore water, and partially buried to retain the heat in winter and stay cool in summer. I was very impressed, here in the US, where I was under the notion that nobody gave a fuck about environmental issues. Then she took me back to Rob's. I fed Jakey, his dog, and settled in front of the tv, nothing that interested me as usual so took to reading a book Maike had given me, a backpacker thriller called Dark Places, by Jon Evans. Made a light meal, and drank a couple of beers before retiring. I was aware of Rob coming in at some point.

A quiet morning waiting for Rob to surface. It was Sunday, so I used my phone card, excellent system and cheap, to talk to Mum and Dad. About eleven, Rob arose, and after some coffee, we went to Rita's for a late morning meal. It was a mexican place, so the food was burritos and tacos, really nice. I had discovered that to get black tea, you have to ask for English breakfast tea, so I was at the counter ordering another cup. This biggish guy with a cowboy hat on was suddenly beside me, and drawled in a threatening voice, "I hear there's one too many limeys in this joint." Staring at me menacingly. A little shiver went up my spine, and I looked down the cafe towards the exit, to see Rob pissing himself laughing and realised the guy was a friend of his. We introduced ourselves, and he came to join us for a chat. Rob was building adobe houses for a living, and he took me to a project that he was finishing up, owned by an Aussie ex rock star called David. I met him and his nephew Rod, who was also coming on our road trip.

He told me that everyone accused him of being British, so Yanks have got the two accents muddled, it's why people keep saying, "oh, you're from Australia." The place was called the castle, and it looked like a castle, huge and sat on a large plot of land.

We drove out to John Dunn bridge, another construction over the Rio Grande, or big river which forms about half of the border between The US and Mexico. Up on top of the gorge, the views were excellent, wide open spaces, and interesting looking geology. Then to Arroyo Seco, or dry creek, a village north of Taos, where another bunch of Rob's friends lived, and I met Brendon, Mark and a few others, chatting and sampling the first of the day now. We had to do some shopping, then to The Alley Cantina, Rob's local, frequented by a mix of clientele, including Native Americans. A great place, but we were only staying for a couple that evening, as Rob was back at work in the morning. A snacky sort of supper and two or three more watching a movie, then quite an early night.

Had a cuppa, then drove Rob to work, the first time driving that big old American truck, automatic gears, a five litre motor, so powerful. Jakey came along with me for the ride, he was an old dog so couldn't walk so far anymore, just a short one for him to take a shit. I got a bit lost on the way back, but recognised a landmark and got back on track. At home, I cleared up and knocked up a small breaky. There were resident mice, a bit of an infestation, so traps were set around and about. I heard one snap with a loud crunching sound. When I looked, the poor critter was in its death throes, so I didn't stay watching it, I felt a bit sickened. In town, I walked it, I found the library didn't open until midday, so I used the cyber cafe instead which cost four bucks for 40 minutes. Went back to get the truck and drove to Taos Pueblo, but it was really expensive to go in, so I gave it a miss. Caught up with the diary, read some National Geographic, performed hygiene chores, and started researching Mexico from the LP. Rob came back early, so we went to the plaza for a coffee and tea, with his workmates Miles and Richard. At the bar we met Roleyn and Brian, and a sound interesting convo ensued. A nightcap at The Alley, with some nachos, chatting to a group of Canadians, then home to sleep.

Diana phoned to say she was running late, which I was relieved about as I felt a bit rough, and savoured an extra couple of teas. Back at hers, I met Josh, and after another drink, we headed about 30 miles out into a forest with their dogs, and towing a trailer. It was winter fuel gathering day, and we spent most of it cutting down dead trees with a chainsaw, taking it in turns, chopping the trunks into manageable sizes to load onto the trailer which had high sides and a back gate. The talk was chunky, lots of opinion about environmental concerns, and I was deeply impressed that they were very strict about only felling fully deceased timber. Great views of the mountains on the way there and back, and we unloaded the firewood at Diana's, then she dropped me back home. Rob went for a beer, but I felt tired, it had been a good work-out, so I just cooked some food and had a couple there, crashing early.

Odds and ends sort of day, started the process of securing a hire car for our road trip. Bit of mailing at the library, read some of the book and NG mag. A couple at The Alley turned into a few. Diana picked me up the following morning, and I went with her to do her recycling round. More engaging chat, and very inspired with what I'm seeing here in The States, collecting everything that can be recycled, paper, glass, metal and plastic etc. Then taking it all to a plant to be sorted and compressed into squares, loaded onto trucks and taken to be made into new goods. Brilliant. Bit of lunch, then finish the round, and get dropped at the car hire place to discover that there's a problem with my credit card. Phoned the bank to resolve it. Now too late to get the car today, so some food and a few at The Alley, playing shuffleboard again.

Rob dropped me at Enterprise, then went to collect Rod. My credit card was declined again! WTF. I tried my debit card and it all went through okay; phew, we have a vehicle. I drove back to Rob's place and him and Rod were waiting for me, so we hit the road. The scenery is dramatic already, around Taos, and we were subjected to more glory as we headed south to Santa Fe then Albuquerque. Rod didn't drive, so me and Rob shared the task of piloting, he was like me, not in any hurry, so all calm, not a great deal of traffic and good banter between the three of us. Westward bound now for Gallop on Interstate 40, shortly after, crossing the state line into Arizona. Some of this road replaced route 66 in the 80s, from the Bob Dylan song.

After Winslow, Arizona, we stopped to look at Meteor crater and the visitor centre. Impressive. Probably the best preserved impact basin on Earth, and caused by a space rock, most likely with lots of iron in it, only 50 metres wide, the occurrence happening about 50,000 years ago. The depression made by the relatively small meteorite is 1200 metres across and 170 metres deep: brings it home to you that we should be investing more in looking out for incoming in the present. Astronauts trained there for the Apollo missions, and, through binoculars, you can see a model astronaut at the bottom, roughly central on the crater floor. Onwards to Flagstaff, where we got a motel room between us, and went for Chinese food from the service station. Rod was a toker, so shared a bad boy with him, then, a bit monged, to the bar, playing pool and darts.

Felt a bit fragile, a dope hangover, which I never get with hash, but Rod was smoking strong green. We had a big breakfast at the diner, so many questions, eggs easy over, potatoes chipped, bacon a little crispy, yes please for mushrooms and tomatoes. English breakfast tea please, thinking that would be it. Toast, yes please. What bread? Rye, wheat, wholegrain or sourdough? I don't freaking know, just two slices of whatever you've got the most of! Felt a lot better after eating that though, the ham was like a gammon steak!

It was Grand Canyon day, so we headed for the entrance, quite a way to drive, but lots of forest and mountain views, and snow on the deck, still being above 2000 metres. Stunning. It's another of Earth's majestic landscapes that your visual senses can't work out and appears to be a massive two dimensional painting. Rod was on holiday, so had skinned up his first of the day, which I declined to share with him. We opted for the flight over, which was $80 each, the helicopter tour was much more expensive.

A magical hour unfolded, from above you can comprehend the sheer size of it, The Colorado river cutting through the gorge, the rapids giving it perspective. We could see the chopper down inside and it looked like a bug from up here, further substantiating the magnitude of the whole canyon. After, we drove to Desert view watchtower, more Awesome scenery and vistas that stimulated the brain chemistry, drinking it all in greedily.

We had decided to stay the night in Gray mountain, but when we got there, it seemed to be a ghost town, so we returned to Flagstaff, but stayed in a different motel that appeared to have good nightlife nearby. We had a couple, then got some fish and chips, had a shower and a short rest, before heading back to the bar that was now sounding lively. When the barman gave us our drinks, he said that they were paid for, and pointed to some guys at the other end of the bar who tipped their hats to us. We went to join them, and we struggled to buy a drink, they wanted to pay for everything, displaying Arizonian hospitality. It was a great night, the band struck up, and the dancing began. The beers flowed non stop, and the chat was fun, and we were made to feel like locals, everybody coming to talk to us, and buying drinks. Shooting some pool or eight ball at some point, with pretty all American girls. In the gents toilets, there were urinals and an open plan bowl for turd dropping. One time I went for a pee, a guy was sitting on the bog with his trousers and pants around his ankles. He engaged me in convo while I was peeing, then started to reel off some paper, at which point I quickly finished and shook, and made a hasty exit. We bunged a wad of dollars at the barman in the end and bought a round, and told him to keep the change. One of those truly legendary nights out.

Another monster morning meal, they eat big here. Rob had done the trip before, so we detoured to go see The Painted desert, very striking and colourful, then through The Navajo Indian reservation. I bought a phone card and called my parents, trying to describe what I was seeing. Cross country to Tuba city, and north to Kayenta, now entering The Monument valley. Really bizarre, extremely mad geological formations, that formed during The

Permian and Triassic: dinosaurs roamed here, and the present day is the results of all those hundreds of millions of years of weathering. A masterpiece of Mother Nature and Father Time. We stopped lots of times to take photos, no end of opportunities. One time, we couldn't restart the car, and after half an hour of puzzling, Rod got in, put his foot on the brake and started her up! A safety feature no doubt. We had all indulged in one of Rod's roll-ups, so were a bit slow mentally at that point. We crawled along a road trying to find the exact point that the picture on the front of an Eagles album was, and I got a photo taken with me in it.

Then through Mexican Hat, look it up, completely outlandish. Hotel California came on the radio, so that got us singing. We had crossed another state line, and now in Utah. We went to Four corners, where you can hop around four different states, Arizona, Utah, Colorado and New Mexico. Further east, you start to see the forested hills and mountains again at Cortez, then a bit of a climb to Durango where we decided to spend the night. Quick shower and change of clothes, then a taxi to the bar area. The first bar had about 100 draft lagers and beers, a bit tricky to choose, and can't remember what I had. I expect Rob had Stella. We got chatting to a couple from Manchester, a small world sometimes. At another bar, I got talking with Amy, an anthropologist, and we all ended up playing pool. The last bar, the shooters were being lined up, but after a couple, I could feel myself sinking, so I walked back, pissed, cold and tired. Rob and Rod came home much later. I'm a bit of a lightweight.

We decided to just get going, and stop somewhere for food, me driving, being the least hungover. The scenery was captivating, the traffic light, but there was nowhere to stop and eat until we got to Pagosa springs, now closer to lunchtime. I had liver and mash, and a lovely cup of English breakfast tea. The mountain pine forest vistas are now the portrait we were being subjected to. Strange how landscapes can change so dramatically, so quickly in this part of the world. Back in New Mexico, Rob and Rod both fall asleep, so I just drove steadily, putting the miles behind us. I stopped to fill the tank with gas, and was astonished how cheap fuel was compared to The UK. Through Chama, then pick up the highway 64, to wind our way through Carson National forest and all its beauty, quite a lot of snow on the verges and woodland floor. Back in Taos, mid arvo, drop Rod off, back to pick up the truck, then got shot of the car. To Smiths for some shopping, got chatting to a lady who heard our accents, and wanted to talk about Australia. We pointed out that we were English, and she was happy to converse about that country instead, which was nice. Back home, we chilled, knocked up a feed, a couple of beers, and a movie before a fairly early night. The mice seem to have multiplied since we've been gone.

Bit of a lie in, Rob had to go back to work; I cleaned up the kitchen, and had some breakfast. Dispose of a few dead mice, shave and floss my teeth, phone Ally and Gina, alls well with the house, the rent was paid on time. Catch up with the journal, read a bit, then walk into town, where I got some children's Spanish learning books, with pictures and the English plus the Spanish words by the sides of them. Put the photos in to be developed, as Rob wants some of them. Back home, I watched Fahrenheit 9/ 11, which I found disturbing if true. Rob was back early, so we had a couple of beers, then his sister Debbie phoned from the UK. She was a bit confused when I spoke to her, not really knowing who I was? Made arrangements for a curry night at Diana's place in two days time. To The Alley Cantina for a few, chatting to a guy called Bruce, then home for a feed and a couple more.

Muesli for breakfast, and the usual teas. Reread the Grand Canyon literature we got whilst we were there. Speaking to my parents on the phone, Dad told me he had a bad flying lesson, he was undergoing private pilot training. Walk to town and collect the snapshots, some decent photos amongst them. Chile line to the Greyhound depot, to enquire about buses to the border. Bit of shopping, a short siesta, then Rob was back, so I borrowed his truck to go get beer. Joe and Julia arrived, Joe was studying cosmic physics, and there was a total eclipse that afternoon: he is a student of Diana's it turned out. A lovely evening of lively intelligent conversation, food, drink and of course the magnificent eclipse earlier. They were telling me at some point that they dumpster dive? It's quite common apparently, the enormous amount of food that gets chucked out by supermarkets, put into skips, is still fine to eat, and some people live off it, seeing it as an environmentally sound way to use some of the thrown away produce. The stores don't like it, and take measures to stop it, but there are ways.

Late up, and clean dishes, have some food and tea. To the plaza, email at the library, and potter around the bookshops, picking up second hand material, getting some I thought Rob and Diana might be interested in. Later, when Rob was ready, we went to Rose and Josh's place and had another thoroughly enjoyable evening of curry, drink and chat. All the misconceptions I previously had about The States, were being debunked one by one. There is a healthy environmentalist movement that walks the walk, not just talks the talk, and Americans are not as stupid as the rest of the world believes them to be. In fact, I met some of the most educated and knowledgeable human beings I'd ever encountered right there in South Western USA. Rob was telling the story of when National Geographic came to town to do a piece on the native Americans, and interviewed him, thinking he was one. He's half Burmese, so has slightly Oriental features, and can speak

Spanish. He dresses like the locals, so it was an understandable error, but he played them along for a while, before admitting he wasn't even from the States.

A bit of a lazy day, checking internet banking at the library, pottering, reading and watching news on tv. I don't like American news, it is very biased and could understand why people in other parts of the world think what I talked about in the last paragraph. Truth is, most intellectual folk wouldn't sully themselves by viewing it except maybe for a bit of local knowledge. There are good papers, not the mainstream ones I'm learning, but there is enough truthful journalism in the US for the facts to be available. When Rob came back, we had a couple of coldies, then later to The Alley Cantina for a full on session, the shots again is what does for me, and I ended up wasted. I think Rob cooked and I might have eaten some, but couldn't actually remember.

It was already afternoon when I woke up, and I felt lousy. I had to skip the recovery teas and food, as I was supposed to go to the station to buy my bus ticket for tomorrow night's passage to El Paso. Hit the cashpoint, then Chile line to Greyhound, and secured my seat for the ride. A Mexican cafe for food and teas, and the recuperation was underway. Back in town, it was a Saturday, there was a rally for the campaign for the upcoming presidential election, and New Mexico seemed to be Kerry/ Edwards. People had signs saying honk for them, which grated on my aching head. Hair of the dog back at Rob's, then to Ogelvie's, chatting to Brian again. Some annoying drunks, being obnoxious, bothered Rob, so we left. At The Alley, we played shuffleboard and ate some chicken wings, then to Adobe bar for the halloween party. Me and Rob, or English Bob, as the locals called him, were the only people not dressed up, telling folk that in the UK, halloween is for children. The costumes were fantastic, Mr Pumpkin head, Inspector Clouseau, and Lurch was working the bar. Everyone who came to chat, I knew, but didn't recognise until they told me who they were. Chatted to a travelling mother and daughter, and looked for Rob, but he was gone. I enjoyed the ambiance of an American halloween for a bit longer, then went back to The Alley Cantina, and got on it, ending up dancing with two girls who were squabbling over me. Back home, pissed right up again, Rob made fried eggs on toast, then I slept.

There was some work that needed doing on the house and garden, and Alex was there to help, so I did a bit, but was hungover again, so made the tea and coffee instead. We went for lunch at the World cup cafe in town. A mad man with a dog was shouting "if the thunder don't get yer, the lightning will." He nicked a pumpkin from a shop and smashed it in the road. The Kerry campaigners were still there, so the blaring of horns was going on. Relaxed and got some Thai food to eat. Phoned Diana to say goodbye, and also to Jennifer next door. Final packing up and Rob took me to Greyhound, where we said our farewells for the time being; it's been great to catch up, and Thank you for hosting me. Talked to a Japanese girl who was going to Santa Fe, then the bus arrived, we boarded and we're off: on the road again. Nothing to see out of the window, as it's dark now, so read some, then manage to get a few hours sleep. In one station, a guy was scrounging cigarettes, so I gave him a couple, knowing what it's like. About 3am, we pulled into the bus terminal in El Paso, now in the state of Texas.

In my imagination, El Paso was an outpost in the desert, a rickety fence line, with a gate swinging on rusty hinges. Immigration officers, both sides of the fence, sleeping in chairs in the shade of a dilapidated hut, booted feet up on the rail, a horse tied up nearby, rifle leaning against the wall. A breeze, with a few howling gusts, moved tumbleweed across the landscape of semi arid, rocky and cactus strewn panoramas. Most likely implanted in my mind by watching Clint Eastwood movies in my teens. It was, in reality, a modern city of over half a million people, connected to Ciudad Juárez, in Mexico, which has a population of more than a million. We had dropped in elevation by about a kilometre. I got a scabby breakfast, and found a taxi, realising it was too far to walk it. The driver somehow managed to avoid giving me a price, and didn't put the meter on, distracting me with conversation. The border crossing was just an easy couple of stamps in my passport, and a receipt on the Mexican side to pay something at a bank in the next few days. He took me to the bus station, then told me the few mile taxi ride was $45! Bastard!

There was a bus leaving for Chihuahua immediately, and luckily, just about had enough money to pay for a ticket. The scenery was more like I described in the previous paragraph now, well, minus the tumbleweed. There were rolling hills in the distance, and the desert scrub which I knew had a lot of life dwelling in the harsh, dry ecosystem. I caught up on some sleep, it's sometimes difficult not to nod off, when you are moving along on a decent highway, lulled by the motion, warmth and low drone of the engine. Nearer Chihuahua, the land becomes agricultural, with livestock, fruit trees and other crops, but little habitation other than the farmsteads. Started to see the city from quite a way out, as it is fairly large, three quarters of a million, and quite spread out, with lots of industrial districts as we moved through to the centre. I walked down the road from the station and saw a hotel, which was reasonably priced, left my pack there, and went to find an ATM.

After I'd checked in, I returned to the station to eat a meal, then a local bus to the centre. There are hills all around, the city built on a valley floor, was very pleasant, fine Spanish colonial architecture such as the elegant looking cathedral. It was bloody cold, a bitter wind was blowing, into November now and the altitude was close to 1500 metres. Strolled about a bit, but the near freezing air currents, drove me to return to the hotel. Bit of email at a net cafe, another bite to eat, and a quiet evening with a book. Watch some tv in Spanish, gotta start to submerge myself in the language, intending to study in Guatemala, before an early night, needing some catch up sleep.

Right, I felt ready to undertake the long haul to Ciudad de México. It was still cold outside, so I put on some warm clothes, checked out and back to the station, buying a ticket for the 10.30am departure. Lemon tea, or té limón, was my new found beverage, so had a couple of them with my breakfast. Mexican long distance buses are fine, of a western standard; and punctual, if that one was anything to go by. Leaving the city, the sun was on my right, so I was thinking we were going north? Hope I'm on the correct bus, maybe there has been confusion with my bad Spanish? No, it was fine, we looped around onto a highway, and were now heading the opposite way. Considerable farmland soon became desert scrub again across the whole landscape. Quite hilly near Chihuahua, but flat now with hills in the distance on both sides, the straight road cutting due south. Small towns to pick up and drop off passengers, sometimes someone flagged it down by the side of the road. Finished Catcher in the Rye, a controversial book in its day, censored for a couple of decades; couldn't see what all the fuss was about. Gen up on Guatemala from the LP. Eventually stopped in Torreón, where we got a short break for a sandwich and a smoke. It got dark, and I reran the whole of my plus year long trip through my mind, incredible amount of travelling done, and my memory seemed in good shape. Some people said I should write a book, but don't think I've got it in me.

Watch the sunrise, managed to get a few hours of shut eye last night. Would have crossed the Tropic of Cancer somewhere near Fresnillo, but I wasn't aware of it. A sign telling me that MC is 159, wasn't sure if it was miles or kilometres, but now back in metric territory it turned out. It became built up quite a way out as this is the main population centre in Mexico, and Mexico city has been the largest in the world. It was truly gigantic, and took an age to reach the Terminal de autobuses del norte. Checked out price for onwards; walked along the road and found a smart looking hotel that was 320 pesos for a night, at the time being 21 to 22 to a British pound. Difficulty working out how to use the safe deposit box in the room. Now 10.30am, and I wanted to go and see something of the city. It has a reputation for theft, so I left most stuff behind, the room seemed very secure. Wallet in one front pocket and some change in the other, a small duffle bag for bits and pieces, such as a camera, cigarettes and water.

Ah, that's better, considerably warmer, now in the tropics, but back up over 2000 metres, so cool at night. Torta de pollo y té limón for a morning meal, then a very crowded bus to the city centre; these are the times you have to be alert to pickpockets.

Follow the LP map to Palacio de Bellas Artes, very grand, then Plaza de la Constitución y Palacio Nacional. Outstanding architecture abounded, but everything was a long way away from each other. I got a jugo de naranja, and smoked a fag, then got on the open top tourist bus, 100 pesos for three hours. It goes around all the famous sights in the city; impressive buildings and monuments galore. Commentary through headphones told you about each one, pretty good for a fiver.

I decided to get on the subway to return to the hotel, I got a map and it was easy to work out, and cheap to use. Bag up front, hand on my wallet, the carriages were packed, as it was now afternoon rush hour. Survived the first two short rides, and now was out of the centre and the human traffic thinned somewhat. Just a few stops to go, and the platform was uncrowded when the train rolled in, I started to relax. The doors opened and people streamed off; suddenly I was being pushed into them, and my arms forced upwards. People scolded me, but I wasn't in control; I wrenched my right arm down, my elbow connected with something hard and I heard a female yelp: I held onto my wallet, feeling a hand in my other pocket. Then I tripped on the carriage floor entrance step, and stumbled forward, banging into the opposite wall. I turned quickly, to see other people boarding the train, and couldn't ascertain who the thief or thieves were, maybe they didn't get on? The doors closed, and the train pulled away. I still had my bag, my wallet, but the other pocket was empty, they'd succeeded in getting about 50 pesos off me. Outside the stop nearest to my hotel, was a bar cum restaurant, so I sat with a couple of beers and some food, reflecting that the experience was worth £2.50. CNN en Español back at the room, trying to listen to Spanish as much as I can. Disappointed that Bush has secured a second term in The White House.

Bit of a lie in, up the road for food and tea, and get a bus ticket for San Cristóbal de las Casas, in the state of Chiapas; leaving at 2pm. Read and relax for a couple of hours, then check out and back to the station. Some confusion, probably me not fully understanding something, but eventually find the bus and board.

The city is truly enormous, and we wound through the hills that surround it; then there it was, the 5500 metre volcanic cone that is Popocatépetl. A very active stratovolcano, and has the potential for devastation on a grand scale. If it blew, there wouldn't be enough time to evacuate 20 odd million people. A short stop in Puebla, then some flatter land for a spell before catching glimpses of snow capped peaks in between breaks in the cloud. Started to climb again, then a beautiful majestic sight confronted me: Citlaltépetl, Mexico's highest peak, an inactive volcano, covered in snow, bright white in the sunlight. Films were being shown, and I watched Anger Management dubbed into Spanish, some crappy kung fu film, then Crimson Tide. At one stop, I chatted to Lorenzo from El Salvador, returning for a visit. Thought we were going to have to push start the bus, but it fired in the end. Some sleep, then Tuxtla Gutiérrez at 2.30am. For some reason, they had the AC on full blast, so I didn't sleep anymore, I was shivering. Real windy mountain roads now, pity I can't see anything, until we finally arrive in SC at about 4.30am.

A taxi took me to The Magic hostel, but no one answered the door when I rang the bell. Another hostel nearby, checked me in and I fumbled around in the dark, not wanting to wake up others, before climbing up onto a top bunk to sleep. About 7am, some people got up and put music on! Chat to a Danish guy who told me that everybody was ill. Went for a walk, liking the town already, seems relaxed and most of the locals appear to be indigenous Americans. Plenty of eating choices, so sit for food and lemon tea, getting to like it a lot now. Net cafe for some news and mail, then go to check out Magic hostel. It was fully booked, but made a reservation for tomorrow in a private room; the dorms are crowded and noisy, I must be getting old. Go for a good old wander around, very pleasant, charming cobbled streets, shuttered low level housing, gaily painted. The central plaza wasn't as spectacular as other places, but it's a small town and the yellow cathedral was nice. Plenty of women and kids selling stuff, no hard sell, but I bought a couple of items anyway.

Sitting in a park, flicking through LP, trying to decide what to do, I opted for the Medicine museum. Strolled there through a poorer part of town, it was quite interesting but the information placards were all in Spanish, so I had difficulty tying up from my English language guide leaflet. Weather wasn't very good, there was constant drizzle, so I went back to the dorm to read for a bit. Later, back out for a late afternoon meal, and a couple of corona beers. Bit of chat with the others in the dorm, but quite a subdued atmosphere, so read some more. Before sleeping, I needed a last pee, so climbed back down the ladder, and fell off, hurting my wrist. People coming and going for hours, music and some loud bangs, made sleep impossible, it settled down in the early hours of the following morning.

Noise kicked off again early, so I got up, collected my belongings, and went to The Magic hostel, where they allowed me into my room straight away. Checked out the building, a most amiable place, with a delightful courtyard to sit around. Still moisture in the air, and overcast, but out to get breakfast and some té negro con leche. Shave and shower, read my NG, and chat to a girl from Cambridge and a Danish guy. The weather improved later, so went to Museo Na Bolom, which had a lot of photos of native Americans from the region. Up the steps to Templo de Guadalope, great views over the town and finally to Cerro de San Cristóbal, with more pleasing vistas. The amber museum was closed, so I went back home and booked the trip to Palenque for tomorrow. Spotted a place to dine earlier, where I got an all you can eat buffet meal for 65 pesos, complimented by a couple of coldies. Picked up a few odds and ends to snack on in the morning. Read and sensible turn in time to catch up on lost sleep, but also because it's an early start mañana.

Up at 5.30am, black tea with milk as the hostel had a kitchen with a fridge. Ablutions, and ready by 6.20, but didn't get collected until 6.45. They had my name recorded as Tulk! Maybe they thought I was incredible? Nice hilly scenery, not any deforestation apparent, seem to be aware of water catchment unlike what I often witnessed in Africa. A breakfast stop, but just tea for me, I'd been chomping on my snacks. Tracey, a Japanese Aussie, sat at my table and we got talking. She was solo travelling also, so we spent the rest of the day in each other's company; intelligent and well travelled for her 25 years. The first major sightseeing stop was Cascada Aqua Azul, beautiful blue coloured waterfalls, which me and Tracey strolled around, chatting and taking photos. These amazing places on our planet, that I'd never heard of until you are brought to them on tours like that one. Cascada Misol Ha, was next, another stunner, and could walk behind it but you do get wet. Luckily, the weather was much improved, quite hot early on, as we are now only about 150 metres above sea level: so dried out quickly.

Then to the main event of the day, Palenque, a Maya medium sized city, dating from BC to about 7 or 800 AD. When it was discovered by Europeans, it was completely overgrown by the jungle, and has since been excavated, but there was much more to do, we were seeing only about 10 percent of it in 2004. There was some obvious renovation and rebuilding underway, but it was engaging to potter around, reading all the information, and got some workouts, climbing the hundreds of steps to the tops of the temples. Tracey was superb company, fully engrossed in the history of the place, and our conversation had no gaps in it. Lots of buzzards or zopilotes, leaf cutter ant colonies, and jumping spiders. About 4pm, we were being rounded up for the return to San Cristóbal. Two kids had fallen into a cave, and a rescue operation was underway. Some sick bastards were charging people 200 pesos to take a peek! Back at 9pm, me and Tracey went for supper together, and had a couple of beers, still jawing away, and we arranged to meet up tomorrow.

Relaxing morning, lovely day, teas and breaky, read and sunbathe. To town for some mailing, forgot to bring the slip to pay my Mexican tourist tax, so had to return to the hostel. Lots of street dogs here, sitting in the plaza waiting for Tracey to show up. We went for a wander around the markets, where there were basic eateries, so we sat down for lunch. Sopa pollo, followed by bistec con arroz. To the bus station to get her ticket for tonight's departure for Mexico city, and that time of day again, so into a licenced cafe for a couple and exchange email. Bit sad saying goodbye, but I think I've got partially used to it now, and we will stay in touch. Very quiet evening, chatting to a Canadian called Pascal. Gets quite nippy at night this time of year, but some heating on inside. A couple hours reading then into the lumpy bed trying to find a comfortable position.

Arise about 6.30, the ladies in the kitchen have been keeping the fire going all night so nice and cosy. Couple teas, then collect stuff, and check out. A cheesy Mexicana type breakfast, very tasty. Feet have got cold, it must be hovering around freezing but promise of a warm day to come. Walk down Insurgents and find the vans going to Comitán, 30 pesos and about one and a half hours. The one to Ciudad Cuauhtémoc was leaving immediately, love it when it pans out like that. A fast drive, so only an hour and 15 minutes, with glorious hilly, tree covered scenery to ogle. Stamped out of Mexico, and share a car to Guat immigration; easy entry with 90 days marked in my passport.

GUATEMALA AND EL SALVADOR.

I chatted to some girls about the chicken bus, and a guy in a vehicle was trying to get us to go with him. Change money at a bad rate; I needed a piss, so I went to find a toilet. When I got back, the girls were gone, but matey was still hovering about, and offered me a ride to Quetzaltenango for 60 quetzales, of which there were slightly under 15 to one pound then, so seemed reasonable. Only me all the way there, and was a little worried as we were in very remote country, though beautiful. He could speak a little English and told me many things on the drive, with stunning vistas and a fast flowing river running below. The villages were much more third world looking than in Mexico, but, again, people seemed happy, well clothed and nourished. The Guatemalans eat big lunches, so we stopped for one half way, and I tried my first Guat Gallo beer. Bit stuffed, we continued to Quetzaltenango, or Xela as the locals call it, pronounced Shala. He dropped me at the Occidental, with okay rooms con baños privado. A shower, and later to the salón Tecún, for four beers and listen to a Queen tribute band. To the market for a light bite, before returning for some sleep.

Ablutions, then down the road for breakfast. Laundry in, go and check out a few of the Spanish schools, and I got a good feel for one, but will think about it for a couple of hours, no haste necessary. Walk around the market area, buying a new fleece, it's pretty cool here in November and at 2300 metres. The Guatemalan women and girls dress in very colourful and traditional attire, the population is predominantly indigenous and mestizo. Volcanes

Santa Maria and Santiaguito loom over the city, very active and overdue for an eruption; you often saw a plume of ash ejected from one or the other. Lunch then a few mails, and suddenly in urgent need of the toilet: an arse cheek clenched walk back. Bit of local adjustment going on there methinks. Collect my clean clothes, and decide to book with Eureka school, so go there to arrange. $110 a week, living with a local family, all meals included and five hours of one to one tuition Monday to Friday; will start tomorrow. This is a very pleasant city, narrow cobbled streets, a nice central plaza, interesting market and people; feel I've made a good choice, can't wait until I can communicate better. Surrounding scenery is tranquil, the volcano a bit of a worry, but it's studied for increases in activity. Will be hiking up to them hills from time to time. Shower and a shave, read a while, then back to Salón Tecún, a good vibe, for a few, then some food at the market stalls, language problems but not for much longer.

Up at 6.30, raring to go. Get a morning meal plus tea, then to the school, where I'm assigned to my teacher Carolina. Basically spend the day learning the Spanish alphabet, not so dissimilar from the English, but the sounds are different. We move on to other stuff for the last hour and my brain is starting to hurt now, and glad when 1pm comes round. The casa Señora comes to collect me, and walks me back to their house, showing me to my room. I was reading signs on the streets, and now I knew the sounds of the alphabet, I could pronounce the words, Spanish being a phonetic language. I might not know what they all meant, but it was a good start, and wondered why my tapes and books from earlier attempts had not shown me this. Seemed totally logical that the first thing to do when studying a new tongue was to know the alphabet? I met Henrik from Sweden at lunch, and the household was grandmother, mother and daughter. I didn't feel confident enough to talk, so just listened, this might be the way to go, total immersion. Whiled away the arvo, by reading and studying. Met Valentine, a dutch guy, who refused to speak any English, so we didn't chat much yet. Had to go and buy bog rolls, as there were none in the bathroom. Cena a las siete, bit more reading then an early night.

Desayuno at 7.15am, Henrik and Valentine chatting away with the family, can understand the general theme of the conversation, but don't say anything, not confident enough yet. Go to school, and a guelling session, straight into the deep end it seems, probably the best way, but quite confused, and walk back to the casa in a bit of a daze. Lunch was ready, but not much said as H and V not there, so I struggled to formulate answers to their questions. It was my fourth meal, and not a sniff of meat, think it is a veggie household? Felt I needed some extra protein for brain food, to help with my studies, I'm gonna have to have a cafe feed in town. First poo, and a shower, agua caliente, thank fuck. It was Friday, so no school tomorrow, but there was an excursion organised amongst the staff, and I had signed up for it. Sneak a meat meal in the parque, and back to escuela to do email, and internet banking. Shop for a few bits for mañana, then home to read about El Salvador, and more study. Dinner at 7pm, then another swotting session. There was a beaker of water left in the bathroom for rinsing teeth, and I adopted that practise there onwards. You dip your brush in to wet it, then clean teeth, and rinse, then swill the toothbrush in the remaining water, thus cutting down drastically the amount you use. It is one of those fine tuning environmental habits that will only be effective if billions take it up.

Early meal, then to school, where there was an English girl and a young lady from Belgium waiting. The guys who were taking us arrived late, because they'd been on it last night, naughty boys. They drove us to the west of the city, then we got in a shuttle van, a mode of transport in Guatemala, to San Martin. We then had a very pleasant hike uphill, through small settlements and maize fields, looking down a valley that was fully forested. Quite steep in places, and I was once again surprised that I seemed to be fitter than the girls who were only in their 20s. It felt like a good workout. At the entrance to the reserve, you pay 15 quetzales, about a quid: another half hour uphill, then a fair walk downhill to the shore of laguna Chicabal. There's a volcano sometimes visible, but the cloud and mist denied us, sometimes shrouding the lake as well, giving it a very mystic, horror movie feel. When the veil parted occasionally, we got superb views across the water, with thick forest growth all around. Sit and chat for half an hour, eating ham rolls, giving some to a stray dog. A long haul back to San Martin, then a very crowded return to Xela. Pollo con arroz late lunch and back to casa for a lie down. Met Daniel, Mama's son, and he showed me some photographs, giving me one as a gift. A night out with the school crowd, watching bands playing Fleetwood Mac and Genesis numbers.

Señora got up to make me desayuno, bless her. I met Adaline, the Belgian girl, about 7am, and we got a van to the bus terminal. We waited on the chicken bus until 8.30, before it got underway. About two and a half hours to Chichicastenango, hilly cultivated scenery, a fair bit of deforestation, but towards and along the tops, the trees were left, so they have the water catchment thing sussed. Quite a few villages, where people get down or get on, sometimes the vehicle becoming jam packed, lots of folk standing. Los Encuentros was a sizable town, then shortly after there, we arrived in Chichi. The market was great, one of my favourites, really traditional, a church with incense burners, and flower sellers.

We both bought stuff, a jacket and shirt for me, and had lunch there, soup and a pork dish. Stalls selling masks, and took lots of photos, which came out well, and already on my computer ready for when I publish. Reckon I must have upgraded the camera, but still hadn't gone digital. Adaline was interested in the political propaganda notices, and took a lot of shots of them. She was a bit strange, morose, and not very talkative. Back in Xela, had a swifty in Salón tecún, then back to la casa to read and get ready for the morning. I engaged in a convo with Valentine, and I think I'm starting to get a grip on this now, he was quite complimentary about my improvements: this coming week will be the turning point I reckon.

Breaky with Henrik and Señora. The lesson today was los verbos: fuck me, it's getting complicated, and more throbbing at the temples by the end of the session. The English girl who came on the walk on Saturday was Heidi, a very friendly young woman and chatted with her at breaktime, in our own language. Bit of chat with Carolina in Spanish for the last half hour, then back home for almuerzo. Some meat at last, chicken, rice and chips, a nice meal. I was starting to talk, and they were very supportive and helpful, giving me praise for my progress. Hot water had been put on, so got a shave and a shower. To town to put film in for developing, ready at cinco en punto, or 5 o'clock, then to school to do email. Had one from Diana, so replied and tapped out mails to Bruce and Tracey. Fart around town to kill time, a funeral procession passed through, they are elaborate in this part of the world. Sit in the plaza people watching, and decide on just the one at Salón Tecún. Collected the photographs and back to the house, they were very good and pleased with how they turned out. Read a bit, study more, then cena at siete, all very routine, Ally and Gina would be thrilled. I'm now getting involved with the talk around the table, it really works this total immersion method of learning a language. Evening spent studying, studying and more studying.

More verbs, verbos, and más verbos irregulares; doing my head in, but gotta stick with it though, feel a breakthrough coming along. Show Carolina my photos, just to bore her for a change. Back for lunch, some meat again, maybe they won the Guatemalan lottery? Henrik was off somewhere, but didn't quite understand. Read about El Salvador, a sort of plan formulating now. Go and watch Impactante at the school, a film about the civil war there, and La hija de la puma. The title means shocking, and it was, a brutal time for this country. Bit of chat with others there, and a swifty on the way home. Valentine catches up to me, and my heart sinks, because we have to converse in Spanish. Same same rest of day, dinner and swot.

Desayuno y escuela. Más verbos irregulares. Arrange with Swiss guy and Adeline for Saturday. A la casa por almuerza. Hygiene chores. Escuela por email, no mucho. Read the BBC environmental pages, mucho interesante. A la casa por estudio pocito. Leave at 6.30pm for Casa Argentina, but get lost and don't find it until 7.15pm. Spend evening with Adeline, food, beer, punch and speeches. Salón Tecún the long way round for uno cuba libra and back to sleep.

Bit groggy. Breaky and school. Carolina wanted me to take the photos for her sister to see. Have a long chat with Carolina after class, and starting to feel a fair bit of progress, it's sort of coming together. Really starting to chat a lot at meal times now, the señoras are very encouraging. Spend the afternoon visiting San Andrés Xecul, a small town north of Xela. It has a bizarre looking church, with a multicoloured façade depicting lots of angel images. We walked to the top of the village, up a steep cobbled road, great views over the town and countryside. There were dancers with masks back in the plaza. We went to see San Simón, a sort of cult, where you give him a cigar and get a wish. I wished to be able to speak Spanish better. Quick drink with Adeline back in Xela, then home to find out that Henrik was leaving tomorrow, so went to meet up with him after dinner. Nice evening, a few other Swedes there, and they might be coming to Bay islands in Honduras where I planned to go for some diving, so we exchanged mail to keep in touch. Late night, and didn't get to sleep until medianoche.

I was a bit tired that morning. Say goodbyes to Henrik, and to school for the last day of the week. The others tell me they are not now going to trek to Santa Maria, so I will go alone. Productive day I think, the breakthrough is upon me, and starting to think a little in Spanish, instead of constantly translating in my mind. Back home for lunch, and a toasty hot shower. Few chores, mail and news, a round of postcards, and shopping for some snacks to take on my hike mañana. A crafty beer in ST, and see Adeline and Chris, a guy from Alaska, so ends up as a few. At the casa I read until dinner, then a feeble bit of study: Valentine came to chat, and as I'd obviously made a lot of progress, he suddenly broke into English, and we had a chunky conversation.

Up at 5.30am, and walk along a road; it was very cold, and only a smattering of other people were about. Round a bend, and see Santa Maria; good, I'm on the right track. A pick up colectivo pootled along, and I jumped on it to the start of the trail. Sit and eat a couple of rolls I made up yesterday, enjoying the peacefulness of that time of day. A small group arrived, and I sort of latched on to them, bit of convo with a couple. After an hour, they stopped for a rest, but I wanted to keep moving, so carried on alone. There were signs when there was a choice of direction, but at one fork, there wasn't, so I waited for the group. A long while seemed to elapse, so I decided on the path to my right. I hiked for a couple of hours, and started to suspect I'd chosen wrongly. A group of people were toiling in a field ahead, and I asked them, and they confirmed I'd come the incorrect way, but it was too late now to double back. Oh well, it had been a good and nice walk, with muchos buenos vistas. Still got a lot closer to the volcano, and had great views of it from time to time.

Plenty of wildlife spotted, including a monkey and many birds such as red cardinals, yellow alondras, a lark species. Hummingbirds, and many insects, bees, hairy caterpillars, silkworms, wildflowers and trees galore. Two men on horseback came down the trail greeting me, then a whole family, the guy riding the single horse and the rest on foot. They had dogs that were wary of me, and numerous sheep in the pastures. I came to a wider dirt track that looked like vehicles went along, so I sat and ate some more food, and smoked a ciggie. Sure enough, a truck bumped towards me, heading back to town, so I jumped up for a spell, other passengers with sacks of goods for the market I assume. I got back down at the village I'd passed through on the way up, and continued the rest of the way to Xela on foot, feeling like I'd had a good amount of exercise by the time I got home. After dinner, I went to join everyone at Salón Tecún, for the first semi session since leaving the States.

Struggled to get out of bed, and missed saying goodbye to Valentine, who left that morning, but at least I talked to him yesterday. Felt rough at breakfast, but the ladies were busy, so didn't have to converse much. Met Adeline and Moui, one of the staff at school, and we had a lengthy walk to hostel Los Vahos that had a sauna. It was really hot inside, so sweated out the alcohol, and had to admit that Ade didn't have a half bad bod in a bikini. Shower, changed into clean clothes and had some lunch, lots of scrounging street dogs, then to the road to catch the bus back to town. Felt better, but still a slight headache. Lots of email to catch up with. A cup of tea in the plaza, then home, for some preparation study, ready for tomorrow. I was given Val's old room, a bit smaller, but at the end of the veranda, and clean sheets on the bed. I went through my photos with señora, and she took them to show the rest of the family. Read and swotted lots, dinner for a break, feeling very comfortable talking by now, almost coming naturally. More revision, and an early night.

Back to the grindstone, going over everything again, to try and embed it into my head. Adeline was sick, bad guts apparently. I'm the only student at the casa now, so just chatting with the girls, sort of hoped that someone else would come to stay. Took my dirty clothes to the laundrette, got a hair trim, and a cuppa at a cafe in the parque. Back to the house to read, write postcards and catch up with the journal. Returned to town to pick up clean garments, a swifty in ST, home for cena, and study into the evening.

Onto feminine and masculine, el, la, las y los. Hazel said she didn't get a major improvement until into her third week, so I'm hoping I will be the same; I want it badly, but still feel there's a further breakthrough coming. I will be in Spanish speaking territory for several more months, so I should be competent by the time I return to the UK. Nice lunch, sweet potato wrapped in big leaves, with a nugget of pollo in the mix; yum. Hygiene chores, including sorting my feet out. Little afternoon excursion with a crowd from school, to the cemetery. Lots of tombs as you'd expect, but they are extremely elaborate, they take honouring the dead very seriously here. Good view of the volcanoes, and a burst of ash exploded out of the side of one of them. Few mails at the escuela, and a couple of late arvo beers with Adeline. Casa in time for cena, and more swotting.

I was trying to read The Old Man and the Sea, by Ernest Hemingway en español. Wasn't getting on well with it, too much looking up words in a dictionary. I could read signs, menus and much more, and was starting to write a little in Spanish, but my main aim was speech, so I decided to give up reading books, just stick to English ones. Lessons were now numbers, telling time, days, months, adding new verbs daily. The irregular verbs were not going to be a big part of my vocabulary, but the useful ones, I memorised. Singular and plural was quite easy, but tenses started to become complicated, and only half got my head around them. I was quite happy that I could now converse with all the basics, and started to think that I might have left it too late in life to ever be fluent in another language. The older brain is more stubborn to this sort of thing, doesn't mean you're not open minded, but children don't question new tongues, just get on with it; the child's brain is more sponge-like. The UK education system didn't take language seriously when I was at school, maybe it's better now? But I didn't get my first introduction to French until I was 12, at high school: then it was only an hour a week.

So, I was into my third and last week, totally worth the effort, as I knew this trip would be greatly enhanced by understanding what was going on around me. An afternoon outing to Zunil, a small town nearby Xela where there was a fiesta to celebrate Santa Catarina. Usual mountain scenery on the bus ride there, and a walk over a bridge spanning a fast flowing river to the town itself. Big veggie market, lots of stalls, some selling plastic toys, and street food vendors. Mucho ruido, noise, around the church where bands were playing traditional music, and people dancing in costumes and masks. A colourful and vibrant ambiance abounded, and we stood and soaked it in for as long as we had; the atmosphere was one of elation and pleasure. On the return journey, I just started speaking with the guy sitting next to me, surprising myself after that it had been natural. There was a stall selling cooked chicken, so I scoffed a couple of pieces, then a swifty grande at ST, before returning for the scant dinner; another evening of study and reading followed.

Thank fuck it's Friday. I was struggling with all the formats of the verbs, the ending changes for I, you, he or she, us and them! Then there's masculine and feminine; bewildering. Had to get some dollars from the bank for going to El Salvador. And a boring rest of the day; read, swot, and staying in on a Friday night! Yawn, yawn. Desayuno about 8am, then walk to calle 4a to ride the colectivo to terminal Minerva. A Guatemala city bound chicken bus took me back to Los Encuentros, and another to Sololá. For some reason I thought the town was Panajachel, the absence of a large body of water should have given me a clue, but I went looking for a hostel before I realised my mistake. Back to the station and finally got to my intended destination. I checked into the extremely pleasant Villa Lupita, with lush gardens. Touch of the shits affecting me, unusual after a no drinking night, but you never know if someone has handled your food with unclean hands, just something that happens from time to time. Burger lunch chatting to a Yank on holiday with his daughter. To the pier, but the boat trips are pretty costly, so don't bother, just a decent walk to Santa Catarina Palopó. Lago de Atitlán was formed by a huge volcanic eruption 80 odd thousand years ago, which collapsed in on itself, to form the depression that slowly filled with water. The average depth is over 200 metres, but the deepest part is over 300 metres. It's gloriously picturesque, with three volcanic cones on the southern shore, that are part of the Sierra Madre mountain range, visible to me from my vantage point. All the volcanoes down the coast of Central America are the eastern fringes of The Pacific Great Ring of Fire. I sat with a cold drink, gazing over the very blue water, before jumping on the back of a pick up that was returning to Pan. Shower, feed, and found a decent looking bar, that was advertising a two for one happy hour. Basically got on it with a Texan in dungarees.

Go for a nice relaxing cooked breakfast, and pot of tea. Stroll to the pier for a photoshoot, then back to collect my stuff and check out, having some problems with the key, and communicate with the hosts in Spanish about it; oooh, listen to me. Colectivo to Sololá, then a bus to the junction near Los Encuentros, and wait for the Xela bound one to happen along. Three gringos got off also, and were heading for Chichi, so told them the bad news that they should have stayed on and transited in LE. A very crowded return to Xela, standing most of the way. A cuppa in the parque, then home to tell the señoras about my excursion. On an impulse, I decided to skive off my studies, and go for a Sunday afternoon drink. Glad I did, I found Henrik, Hazel and Adeline in the bar, and had a nice couple of hours jawing with them. A bit squiffy, I walked back with Hazel, she was staying somewhere nearby to me, and met a new arrival. Joanne, a young Swedish blonde, could speak good Spanish and was there to improve towards fluency. So a nice cena with interesting convo, which I was now quite comfortable with. Spent part of the evening talking with her on the balcony, reasoning that was as good as swotting over books.

Last three days of classes, imperfect tense and future tense, stuff is sinking in nicely. To casa for lunch, shave and shower; talk was almost instinctual now. I did a photoshoot of the family, never did write down their names strangely, and went back to town to put the film in for development. Bit of shopping, to school for email and news; saw Adeline and we ended up going for a beer. She wasn't having much luck finding volunteer work for some reason. Quiet arvo reading and starting to prepare a speech that I have to make on my last day.

Joanne started speaking to me in English at breakfast which was frowned upon, not considered polite, so I answered in Spanish, and she twigged. We walked to school together, a very pleasant and attractive young lady. Verbos futuros irregulares. Aaaaaghhhh. It was Neil's birthday, Hazel's boyfriend, who had fucked his foot up, and was having classes at home. At break time, we all went there to give him a cake and sing happy birthday, which took an hour, so a bit of a skive off the intense learning. Just an hour and a half till 1pm, and tomorrow was my last day. Saw Ade, and she finally secured a volunteer position. Joanne and señora were talking about Xmas at lunch, I was proud of myself, I understood the whole conversation perfectly. I had to go to town, and needed some meat, so a couple of pieces of fried chicken; it had reverted back to vegetarian at the house. Posting the photos back to the UK was quite expensive, I obviously kept the film roll in case they didn't make it. Got into some environmental websites after doing email. Swifty at Salón Tecún, and to la casa, for a spell of reading, cena a las siete. Joanne invited me to the cinema, but, unfortunately, I needed to finish writing my speech. We had a chat on the balcony when she returned, before retiring early yet again.

Reiterate three weeks worth of study in five hours, my head was hurting, but I had survived that torture, and could speak passable basic Spanish now. I got a certificate, and had to make my speech, which I kept short and sweet in the end.

"Antes de asistir a la escuela, sabía cuatro palabras en español. Hola, gracias, por favor y cerveza." Which satisfyingly got a smattering of titters. "Ahora, sé muchas palabras. Gracias Carolina por tu inmensa paciencia."

Schools out for summer. Schools out for everrrrr. Had a good chat with Neil who had come along on his crutches to listen, a nice guy and had a huge desire for travel like me; we talked about visiting the Central Asian Stan countries. Home for lunch, chatting away with the ladies continuously, they were impressed with my progress. Shower and shave, and have to go to the laundrette to wash and dry my clothes. Final use of computers at school, and up together with mail, so scan the news. There was something on tonight, so after dinner, me and Joanne went to meet her friends, Hazel and Henrik, Adeline no show. Few too many, walked Hazel home at some point, and back to drink, chat and a little smoke was doing the rounds, so it became quite a big night in the end.

Had my last breakfast with my wonderful hosts and Joanne, with a bit of a hangover. Goodbyes and hugs, then colectivo to Minerva, and a chicken bus to Guatemala city. Dozed quite a lot, but the usual glorious scenery that is prevalent in that part of the world. I just went to the nearest hotel which was $25 for an okay room, with bathroom and tv, including a porn channel. Walked to the centre, volcán Pacaya looming large in the near distance, another active one. Fine architecture, in the Spanish colonial style, that is widespread throughout Latin America, but the air smells pretty polluted. I tried to suss out the bus terminals, but with no luck, couldn't find where transport to San José went from. Guat city has a reputation for violent crime, so not a good idea to be on the streets after sunset. So I got back near the hotel for a feed in a little local place and a couple of beers, chatting to the lady owner/ cook/ waitress. Bit of tele, and an early night.

Quick breaky of tortillas from some girls making them on a street stall. Collected bags and started to walk in a southerly direction, jumping on a colectivo, until it turned right, and continued on foot, miraculously finding myself on the correct road. This is where being able to communicate with the locals is priceless, and some guys stopped the San José bus for me, which was rammed full of people. Lots of stopping and starting before terminating, and easily found the one to Cuilapa. Fully forested mountains, not much cutting had taken place, and hoped it stayed that way. The small areas of agriculture, somehow seemed wholesome and organic; cattle and horses most likely provided the fertiliser, doubt if there is any chemical usage there. A banana milkshake whilst waiting for the next to Valle Nuevo, and more of the same sort of scenery on those back roads. Pick up trucks were ferrying folk to the frontier, an exit stamp, and a walk across the bridge over the Rio Paz, then an entry mark into El Salvador, all very lax. Bus to Las Chinama, and another to Ahuachapan, then a final bendy switchback drive to my intended destination of Tacuba. I got directions to Manola's place, and was welcomed into a homely hostel by Manola, his parents and a Dutchman called Jurgen. Chat a while, then a shower, and we all went for dinner then to a local bar for a skinful. Manola knew everyone, and we were received by the locals with great hospitality. A lot of the local policemen drank there, and something I noticed is that they opened the cigarette packets from the bottom! I enquired as to why, and was told that washing hands wasn't practised after using the toilet, and it was a way of preventing germs getting on the filter tips.

El Salvador has had a violent past also like many Latin American countries, and a lot of travellers skip it because of its reputation. But, I'm finding already, as with a lot of places with ill repute, that it is unfair, and I was experiencing an extremely warm welcome from the Salvadoreños. Desayuno was a family affair, and I noted that Jurgen was using vamos a y voi a before verbs, and not changing the ending, which seemed wrong to me. I asked him about it later and he explained that it was a slack way to say I'm going to or we're going to, and you don't need to change the verb ending. Oh, what a revelation, and me being a bit lazy with such things, adopted that straight away.

We were off to the beach, but it's a long way, so we got the bicycles in the back of the truck, and headed for the beginning of the trail, through fincas and forest country. What a glorious four hours of downhill cycling along the Guatemala border, with the Peace river running to our right, and thick, lush jungle, full of birdlife, including raptors, and many lizards. We had a couple of breaks, and feeling sweaty, we went for a cool off in the river pools, all seemed fresh, clean and virginal. Manola was bumping along behind us in the vehicle, and at our lunch stop in a tiny village, he put several 2 litre bottles of cloudy liquid in the truck. We continued onwards, and shortly were at our digs for tonight, a basic dwelling right on an idyllic beach. The settlement was Garita Palmera, situated on the shore of the vast Pacific ocean, and as remote as you could ever imagine.

A half hour swim, then dried off and changed clothes, ready for the party that was looking very likely by now. I went with Manola to shop, but the first port of call was a bar, so we had a couple of beers, talking to his friends; absolutely fantastic to be able to get involved in those conversations. We picked up supplies, and back to base, where everyone else was now starting to drink. The moonshine in the bottles was called chicha, local homemade stuff and tasted a bit fruity and didn't seem very strong, as we were all supping away and chatting animatedly. I got up to go to the toilet, and my legs didn't want to work properly, so I laid off it, sticking to beer for now. The fresh fish was barbecued, the rice and beans cooked, and a great authentic meal followed. Me, Russ and Elsa from South Africa, Gena from Italy, and Manola plus other Salvadoreños, got a fire going, and some music started up from the truck cd player. The beer, ron and chicha circulated into the evening, and everyone was dancing round the blaze on the beach. At some point, I walked a way down into the pitch blackness, and laid out staring at the beautiful night sky: crystal clear and overflowing with stars. Muy buenos dia y noche.

An easy Sunday morning, feeling rough and still a bit tired, as late to bed last night. Drank loads of coconut milk, and had a dip in the ocean, before a morning meal materialised. The others are staying here for another day, so it was just me, Manola, and his helper, returning to Tacuba, the bikes in the back; would have been tough cycling uphill on the rocky trail. Lovely peaceful drive, a bit bumpy, but our surroundings were superb, and the conversation decent, as it turned out Manola could speak reasonable English, so we got onto deeper topics; I wasn't at that level in Spanish yet. Back home, Jurgen asked if I wanted to go see the parakeet tree, so we hiked a fair way out of town and sat in the shade of another árbol nearby to the 600 year old one that we had come to view. Shortly, a few green birds arrived, perching in the branches, and squawking away, then a few more, lots more, and eventually hundreds, maybe 500 plus parakeets, making a hell of a racket. But it was a spectacular wildlife sighting. Dinner back at the casa, and to the same bar with Jurgen and Tomas. Played pool and drank, the police chief was worse for wear, and another drunk was giving us a hard time, so we left.

Bit of a lie in, no real rush today. Say goodbyes to others off on the bike trip, and play with the kittens, whilst breakfast is being prepared. Eat that, and pack up, chatting to Manola, and pay my dues; Jurgen might be in Bay islands also, so exchange mail. To the bus stand, and a short wait before the chicken bus for Ahuachapan comes along, the same journey of windy roads in return. The bus to Sonsonate traverses la ruta de las flores, the road of the flowers. Beautiful flowering trees and shrubs, meadows full of wild blossoms, with tree covered hills in the distance, including some volcanic cones. Pretty, gaily painted little settlements along the way, everyone smiling and happy in amongst this slice of charm and loveliness. Caught another bus to San Salvador, El Salvador's gun riddled capital city. When I saw a sign to Cerro Verde, I got down and hitched a lift with a truck to a junction, then waited for the bus to El Congo. A short walk to Hostel Amacuilco, nicely situated on the shore of Lago de Coatepeque. Order dinner, hygiene chores, try the computer but too slow, so give it up. Bit of diary writing, so glad I kept up that practise, and chat to a guy from Chile. Couple of coldies, and a feed, then a few of us went to a local bar, including an Israeli who had been to Santa Ana today.

Ordered breaky for 7am last night, but it wasn't ready until gone half past, so now in a rush. The bus at 8am was on time, and took us back to the junction where we found another to the car park at the start of the hike, a switchback drive climbing up, the views becoming superb. A local guide was hired, and me, an Austrian guy, a German girl and an older Spanish man started the walk a little downhill to begin with. My lingual ability was the second best in that group, which made me happy. We met two Americans, one was a peace corp volunteer, and they tagged onto our small group. A decent hour and half uphill hike commenced, the panoramas getting more stupendous the higher we got. The last bit was a scramble up to the lip of the caldera, loose volcanic rock and shale slipping beneath our feet, to make it difficult to finish the ascent. The sulphurous smoke that was engulfing us was quite choking, but a real pleasure to peer into the crater of the highly active volcán Santa Ana. We sat a long while, staring out and about us; our planet really has the ability to stun our brains. Volcán Izalco was even more active, one of the most restless in the Americas. It stood a short way away, cone shaped, and covered with recent pyroclastic material giving it a barren look.

Felt the need for a bit of convo in English, so hiked back down with the Yanks, who were Peace corps and missionaries, so I kept my mouth shut about my religious views. They had a vehicle, so we got a lift back to the hostel, talking about travels, politics and the importance of education,(not of the gospel type in my opinion.) Bite to eat, and still restless, so tried to go for another short hike, but got on the wrong bus, and by the time I realised, it was too late to rectify, so just walked back casually, enjoying the surroundings. Hot and bothered, cold shower, crack open a beer, and chat to a Swiss couple and a German guy. There was a storm brewing, so I read in the dorm which I had to myself. It developed into a cracking tropical tempest, with great fork lightning. A couple who had been camping, decided to upgrade, so they took beds in the same room as me.

After eating, paying the bill and checking out, I got on a bus that I thought was going to San Salvador, but it ended up in Santa Ana,

El Salvador's second largest city. I had to get some cash, stored my bag in the station, and went for a stroll around, an elegant city, with great architecture around the central plaza. On the bus to Apopa, people were telling me that SS is not particularly safe for foreigners, so I thought fuck it, and decided to head north. It was a nice day, travelling through the countryside of ES, talking with the locals and admiring the scenery, which was attractive, mostly rural, and plentiful colour in the nature and the housing. Aguilares looked a bit of a dump, so just stayed on all the way to Chalatenango, the conductor not charging me extra for some reason. A bridge over the Rio Lempa, to the right is where it pools into what looked like a sizable lake. Lots more hilly country before arriving mid arvo, and went to the hotel San José, getting a basic room for $7. El Salvador uses the US dollar as a currency by the way. Nice cold shower, but the room smells musty, then to the parque centro, where there is a bright white cathedral. The national dish in ES is the pupusa, a cornmeal flour flatbread, cooked on a hotplate, and stuffed with different ingredients. A great and cheap way to nourish yourself ongoing. So that evening I ate several pupusas queso, or cheese, from the local pupuseria, along with a couple of pilsner beers, that are sold everywhere. A ceremony at the church, concluded with a loud and dazzling firework display. On the way home, I stood and watched a mixed gender basketball/ netball game and a girl who had quite amazing football skills. Got a bag of chips and back to the room.

A local cafe for breakfast after ablutions. To the stand for buses to San Salvador, doubling back from yesterday to the junction at Amayo. The bus heading north was across the road, so ran to get on, and away almost immediately; nice when it works out like that. Winding up through the hills, climbing half a kilometre, for an hour and a half, usual forested landscapes stretching out and about. Chicken buses are old American school transports and designed for children, so your knees are butted up against the seat in front. Common courtesy and tolerance are usually practised, but the guy next to me that day wanted more than his fair share of room, so I was a bit squashed; I just endured, knowing it wasn't for long. I got down in La Palma, I'd chosen the hotel Pital from the LP, and walked there following the map. It's set down a narrow side alley, in a quiet part of an already quiet town. The rooms were massive, and well furnished, with a plush bathroom, tv, and a covered patio with a hammock hooked up; it even had a swimming pool. At $10 a night, it is probably still the best value for money accommodation that I have ever had, so just checked in for two nights.

It was still early, so went for a stroll, seeing the whole settlement in about half an hour flat. I stopped for a jugo de fruta, y pollo con arroz almuerza. Back to the chateau for a lazy arvo, reading in the hamaca. Did a bit of Spanish revision, but I'm quite happy with what I have now. I can converse about all the basics, and will just have to wait to talk about deeper issues, when I meet people with good English. In the past when I heard people on public conveyances, speaking to each other in a language I didn't understand, I always thought that they were covering profound subjects, but, from what I've heard so far, most folk are just exchanging information about their families and friends. It became beer o'clock, so went to get a couple to drink on the veranda. Decided on a nice rooftop restaurant for the evening meal, with pleasant views over the quaint town and countryside. Kids happily playing a range of games in the streets of little traffic, and all seemed well with the world. A decent feed, and a couple more coldies, then back to my palace for a bit more reading and curl up in the extremely comfortable double bed.

Breaky at the hotel restaurant was decent, but nowhere serves black tea; so pleased I keep a small packet of t bags in my luggage. At the stand, a drunk was pestering me for money, it was 9.30am! A bus to the very pleasant village of San Ignacio, and began to hike to Rió Chiquito, about 8.5 kilometres away. A telecoms lorry came by, and I hitched a lift with it, chatting to the workers, feeling pleased with myself that I can just do so quite naturally now. A moderate walk on a moderate gradient, less than a couple of hours to the summit of cerro El Pital, with grand views over the Reserva Biologica. Lots of young people on the way down, maybe a student outing? Rest a while, then I trekked the cloud forest trail to La Peña Rajada, and actually now in Honduras, the border between the two countries runs through the reserve. I saw a guy who was on the bus yesterday, riding a horse, so said hola and had a few words. Back down to the beginning of the track, and sat with lunch at a cafe in Rió Chiquito, jawing with some locals, my Spanish improving all the time.

The pick up that I hitched a lift with back to San Ignacio, had three girls in the back accompanying me, to chat with, my lucky day. A vehicle was stopped by the side of the road, so we pulled over to help, they'd suffered a puncture, so the driver got stuck in to assist changing the wheel. It was a minibus containing a small circus troupe, including two clowns in their costumes. Whilst the work was being done, they gave us a very funny performance to entertain us in thanks for aiding them. It was one of those bizarre, totally unexpected occurrences that happen from time to time when travelling around the world. I wrote about it on the LP Thorn tree forum, but can't find it now, probably just too long ago, stuff most likely gets taken down after a certain amount of time. The truck was going through La Palma, so I jumped down, giving the driver a dollar, and back to my luxurious suite to read and relax. Grabbed a swifty to sup on the balcony, then got cleaned up and changed. Down the road to eat and drink a couple more, chatting to a guy from Nicaragua, with whom I struggled to understand completely.

It was approaching mid December, and I had decided I would spend Xmas and New year in Bay islands to do some diving and party a bit. I wanted to visit Copán ruins en route, but there wasn't a direct way to get to them, so that day was going to be a long travelling one. I got breakfast down the road, as the hotel restaurant didn't open until 8am. Checked out and to the bus stand by 8.30, another drunk asking me for money. Shortly at the border crossing at El Poy, some confusion with signs, but queued and got my exit and entry stamps done, and onto the next transport.

HONDURAS AND NICARAGUA.

In Nueva Ocotepeque, the chicken bus to La Entrada was almost ready to depart, so we got going straight away luckily. It was a long and windy road, uphill then back down the other side, over and over again, natural landscapes, lots of forest cover and some agriculture amongst the greenery. I'm enjoying the travel here in Central America, seeing that the region is largely intact, not so much land given over to farming yet, populations are fairly stable, so there shouldn't be too much pressure on the nature for the foreseeable future.

Changed bus for the last time that day, and another lengthy meander through Honduras's pretty countryside. A grass head got on, he was singing and clowning around, in a good humoured way, which made people smile. We passed through and stopped in a number of small rural villages, and the territory traversed was rolling hilly, tree covered panoramas, some cultivation going on obviously, but, again, it seemed organic; there must be much wildlife living in the midst of all that jungle. Copán Ruinas town was reached about 5pm, and I went to the hotel Los Gemelos, checking into a pleasant room, with shared bathrooms, but it was a very cheap option. Email was piling up, so I did a spell in the internet cafe, swifty and a great steak feed, before a few more in the bar. Tiredness got the better of me by 9pm, it had been a long day, so back to sleep early.

A simple breaky of toast with butter and jam, plus tea, before walking out to the ruins. I started with a nature hike, abundance of flora, tropically lush, spider webs across the paths, so I must have been the first that day. Birdsong everywhere, and spied a few colourful avians flitting between the branches, too fleeting to identify species. Too many mosquitoes, and wished I'd brought my repellent stick. At the entrance, there were three guys in combats, toting rifles. Scarlet macaws perched in trees and agoutis browsed the undergrowth. Many more pretty birds, wasps nests, other insects and arachnids were plentiful. Another fine example of how nature will fight back against human occupation, lots of reclamation by big trees growing through the buildings, like at Angkor Wat. Slight interest was taken in the site back in the 30s, and a river was diverted to save what was left of the eroded acropolis. It attained world heritage status in the 80s, and recent increases in tourism has made excavation worthwhile. But I was seeing it in its earlier stages of that process, and it was a delight for me to once again observe Mother Nature's ultimate power over us sapiens.

Las Sepulturas was less than two kilometres away along a trail with thick vegetation and established trees. It was where the Maya nobility lived, the buildings more elaborate, but also in the early phase of archaeological uncovering, and I was more fascinated by the overgrowth, it just gave the site an eerie feel. I saw many birds, wished I'd recorded species, squirrels, more agoutis and macaws. A family was wandering along the river bank, and to the bridge; it was a lovely rural setting, the air oxygen rich. A stroll back to town along the road, feeling at peace, and looked around the settlement a little more. Cobbled roads and buildings with tasteful street art, The Latinos seem to love colour. The graceful and ornate plaza, the church always the best kept edifice in most towns. Bit of internet time, continuing to catch up on mail, news, and doodling a bit, the speed is quite good, so get things done. Cuppa sat outside a cafe, people watching, lots of bars and restaurants. Eat food bought from the pavement vendors, baleadas are tortillas filled with a variety of savoury ingredients such as beans, cheese and a creamy sauce; and are very tasty. A few in a bar chatting to the friendly locals.

Right, time for some diving. Toast and tea, check out and to the bus terminal. Return to La Entrada reasonably quickly, and the San Pedro Sula one was nearly full, so away smartish. The roads were not bad, so we were cantering to galloping mostly. I was chatting with two guys, constantly trying to practise my Spanish. José helped me find the bus for La Ceiba, I was relieved to be out of SPS, it has a bad reputation for violence. The vehicle was nicer than chicken buses, like a coach, still old, but definitely more leg room, and we made good time getting there. A taxi driver quoted me 100 lempira to the port, about three quid at the time, so I started to walk, and another came and said he would take me for 50, as he already had one passenger. So I made it there in time for the 4.30pm crossing to Utila, literally jumping on as it was departing. I went to the top deck for a smoke and met Willy John from Ireland, who worked as a dive instructor in Utila, and was just completing a visa run. We hit it off straight away, and talked for the whole hour, before taking me to some basic digs near his dive shop. A clean up, great pork kebabs for dinner and a few with the dive crowd at a place right over the water, with views out to sea; felt something like a homecoming.

Up early and out for breakfast, there was a shop filling water bottles and containers, so got some refills done. Laundry in, and internet to let Jurgen and Henrik know that I'd arrived. I wanted to rent a house, but it will only be cost effective if I can sublet the second bedroom. Check out some that were available, one is great if some of the Xela crowd are coming. Good scout round the local area including the beach, and chat to Mathew and Tex at the dive shop, and book a couple for tomorrow, eager to get back into scuba. Tried to relax and siesta, but the mosquitoes and sand flies were relentless. The shower was shit, cold water and barely a dribble. Collect clothes and check mail again, perfect, people are on their way. A feed and a coldie before joining the divers at Bundos having a farewell drink for one of the instructors leaving.

I'd bought cereal and milk, and left it in the shared kitchen, but it didn't open until 6.45am, so it was all a bit rushed, taking away the notion of a relaxing morning. Sand flies are a big part of life here, someone gave me baby oil, must get a bottle for myself. Collected gear and to the boat, and out to Diamond caye for my first dunk in nine months. Corals are reasonably healthy, sea fans, scorpionfish, lobsters and lots of fish fry, though not an abundance of reef fish. At Labyrinth, there were some dead patches of coral, but not too bad. More reef fish, such as butterflyfish, blue tangs and parrotfish; and a toadfish, an ugly looking critter, an evolutionary novelty. Got lunch at Mama's, and made the decision to take the house. It was cheaper for a month, so fuck it, I'm staying for a while. Got the cash, and read for a while, chatting to Willy John at one point. Moved in at 3pm, and got some provisions, food and booze. Mail Jurgen and Henrik, and watched tv for a spell, it had sky, so some documentary channels. Cooked and drank indoors, I seem to have a cold coming on; great, just in time for diving. The congestion caused by having a cold makes equalising more difficult.

A rooster had its perch on the ledge right outside my bedroom window! I was abruptly awoken by loud crowing at 4am. I tried to shoo it away with a broom, but when I laid back down, it just came back and cock a doodle dood again. I'd booked diving, but I was tired, and it was pissing down. My immune system had worked its wonders, along with some garlic I ate last night, and my cold never really materialised. The rain eased, and I decided to go diving. It was cold on the boat, but the warm Caribbean sea was lovely. Glad I came, turned out to be a great day, nice corals, and sea fans at Rocky point, and lots of interesting small stuff. Porcupinefish, barracuda and a burfish, which has weird characteristics. Ted's point was a small wreck dive. Two big lobsters under the hull, a green moray eel, stingrays swimming by, garden eels, cleaner shrimp, goldentail moray and a scrawled cowfish, aliens galore. Brittle stars and lots of good coral, and an octopus hiding in amongst some.

Back at Cross Creek dive shop, me and Willy went through the books, to identify anything we were unsure of. He was a good guy, passionate about conservation efforts being more robust, so as to actually protect the wonders of the deep. Had a conch lunch, but was told later that I shouldn't, they are becoming rare with the overharvesting of them. A round of postcards, read, sand flies and mossies are about, so burn a coil, which the mosquitoes seem to like! Watch some old American sitcoms, and am reminded why I don't watch much tv. Went to eat at Bundos, chicken wings, spuds and salad. A few beers with the crowd, not using my Spanish much, everyone speaks English. We went to see a band playing at Tranquilas but it was quiet, so just the one and back home for a nightcap, out on the balcony, smoking a one skinner from some weed I'd obtained earlier; pleasant little stone to sit on and think about the world, life and the universe, before tiredness got the better of me.

The cockerel kept me semi awake, but it stopped at some point, and I had a lie in to catch up on sleep. There were bird feeders hanging up below the veranda eaves, and I saw that morning that they were specifically for hummingbirds. Something very special about seeing such beautiful creatures at close range, including the startlingly stunning ruby throated hummingbird. After breakfast, I reckoned on a walk. The first path I went along led to the island's landfill site, wishing I hadn't seen that. I doubled back and picked up the other fork, which took me across the island to the small airport. A light aircraft landed as I hiked along the fenceline to the coast. A trail of leafcutter ants, fascinating how big the load they carry is compared to their body size. Shellfish and other marine organisms in the rock pools, and lots of green lizards and snails in the vegetation above the craggy shore. On the way back, I stopped to watch big blue crabs in the muddy marshes beneath a copse of trees. A larger crested lizard shot over my path ahead of me back near the town. Bit of a siesta, and will have to stay in tonight. Knock up a feed, and have beers and weed, but the tv programming was shit, and the commercial breaks long and far too regular, annoying as fuck.

A casual morning, nice to have your own place with all the facilities, and an agreeable view sat out with a cuppa, loving the hummingbird activity. The weather channel on tv covered the US only annoyingly. Jurgen is on his way and will take the spare room in the house for a week, excellent, can relax a bit on my budget now. A rare mail from Marc about a mutual friend, Yeah man Paul. PADI are struggling to take payment from my account for renewing my DM subscription, sort with the bank. Weather looks changeable over the coming days. Nice chicken soup lunch, endeavour to have at least one Spanish conversation each day, and already feel a little rustiness creeping in. Wet arvo, so watch tv and read. Later go to see if anything is happening but think everyone is saving it for Christmas now. Get a small meal and a couple of beers, then a quiet evening at home.

I had half heartedly asked around about dive guide work, but it is very low pay, most of the DMs are local guys, trained up and work for peanuts because it is better than working for chicken feed in agriculture. I'm coming to the conclusion that if I want to be a dive professional, I will have to do an instructors course. It costs about 2 grand US, and my visit to Utila more or less determined that I had definitely left it too late in life for employment in the dive industry. Two tanks there was $35, so I just relaxed, and enjoyed the underwater world and forgot about trying to forge out a vocation in recreational diving. I now have a way of earning money back in the UK, and quite enjoyed being home for the summer months, and the banter on a building site.

The two dives that morning were just me and Brooke from the States, a young lady already an instructor which just confirmed my ruminations already discussed. At stingray point, we logged a hawksbill turtle, two lobsters, one enormous, nudibranchs in soft corals, fairy basslets, a drum fish, another strange critter and hogfish. There was someone selling burgers on the beach at our surface interval on a cay, so, feeling peckish, I chowed on one. Stingrays feeding on our second dive, lots of attractive corals and sea fans. A juvenile drum fish, quite different from the adult which is common amongst reef fish. Grey angelfish, queen angelfish and quillfin blennies. A good walk in the afternoon to the north of the island as the weather was much improved. Do some cooking for myself, but it doesn't really work out cheaper, and you have to shop, prepare, cook and, worst of all, wash up. I hooked up with Willy John and a couple of others for a pub quiz at Bundos, which we won, but put the winnings behind the bar, getting a free drink for ourselves. Someone had completed their divemaster training, and had to drink through a snorkel, with a mask on, so couldn't breath through his nose. It seemed to go on for too long, before he ripped it all off, gasping for air. He was pretty arseholed.

The rooster woke me at four, got up for a pee, and drank a load of water, feeling a bit hungover. It shut up by about six, so back to sleep and woke late, but quite refreshed. Went for brunch and chatted to a couple of American chaps from Denver. Things were panning out, Henrik not coming until 29th now, which fits in perfectly with Jurgen being here. It was pissing down, so spent the arvo indoors reading, and finished off some leftovers for an early dinner. Went to the ferry port to meet Jurgen, and took him to the house, where we caught up over a couple of beers. After he had settled in and showered etc, we went to Tranquilas, and met up with a Swiss guy and two Canadian girls who Jurgen had met in San Pedro. Was offered some bar work, but declined, no real need now that I can sublet a room in the house. Turned into a good but late night.

It was nice to have some company in the morning, we talked about rent and he was very happy with $40 for the week, I'd paid $300 for the month. He wanted to cook, so I popped out for some supplies; he knocked up some tasty egg and cheese on toast. I had to see the owners about a few fixes, and I mentioned the cockerel, but they told me he was Xmas lunch, so only had to put up with it for a couple more days; felt a bit guilty that I was now listening to dead rooster crowing in the morning. Jurgen wanted to do his advanced course, so I went with him to book it. Bit of nosing around a few shops, then a fish burger lunch at Mama's. Fancied going snorkelling, so got some kit, and waded out to a shallow reef through some sea grass. The corals didn't look in great shape there, but lots of life, parrotfish, surgeons, a shoal of juvenile barracuda and a spotted eagle ray. Jurgen cooked spaghetti and veggie sauce, and we just had a couple as both diving tomorrow.

Two nice chilled out dives with a surface interval on one of the many cays. At spotted bay, we had excellent visibility, really attractive hard and soft corals, two big barracuda, a green moray, and a rather large porcupine fish. Big rock also had beautiful corals, looking healthy and abundant making for a terrific landscape. Purple trunk coral, cleaner shrimps, cowfish and nudibranchs are the other notables mentioned in my log book. It was one of those special days, sunny, and good company, marvellous activities, and even some joke telling on the way home with the skipper and mate. Jurgen did alright with his refresher and has started advanced training. Fish lunch, then phone home, speaking to Mum and Dad, then Ally afterwards. There is a big night arranged, so get another feed in, then sample the first coldie of the day; yup, it went down well. A pub crawl followed and the occasional joint was being passed around, so got quite mellow. We ended up at The Bar in the Bush, a rough spit and sawdust local establishment. Two guys were having an argument and pushing each other around, so I thought I could talk some sense into them, being in a happy and harmonious mood. They didn't take kindly to my intervention, and I got knocked down, leaving me with a split and bleeding upper lip; I still have the scar to prove it.

I hadn't done a very good job of cleaning up my face last night before crashing. There was blood on the pillow, and I finished the process after some teas and fags. Probably should have got a stitch put in it really, but, well, you know, I was....well, I couldn't be bothered. It was already afternoon, so I went and got a big lunch at Tranquilas. Lots of sand flies, so lathered up with baby oil. My lip was sore, and I treated it with antiseptic cream, last thing I needed was an infection. There was a little cinema, and they were advertising a showing of a recent movie called The Terminal, starring Tom Hanks. Quite liked him as an actor, so versatile in his roles. So that was how I spent the evening, pretty good film.

Finally got to dive on the north side, bit of discomfort with the mask pressing against my cut lip, but the salt water will do it good. Koos, a dutch instructor and I had two pleasing dives, at Jack's Bight and Rebecca's garden. Not much recorded in my log book, good healthy corals, a big green moray and free swimming nudibranchs. We had difficulty navigating back to the boat after the first dive apparently. In my journal, it says there were not many fish but got an explanation from Phil back at the dive shop. Something to do with migration for breeding purposes?

After lunch, I went to the internet cafe to learn about an atrocity committed in San Pedro Sula. A criminal gang had shot up a bus full of Xmas shoppers including kids! 28 people, 4 of them children, were killed in the savage massacre. It was apparently a warning to the police to back off the drugs bust purge that they were attempting to undertake. Anyone who was going back to the mainland soon, were changing their plans, and it put a bit of a damper on Christmas eve celebrations. I met up with people at Bundos, then Tranquilas and later to Coco Loco for a subdued party.

Nice lie in, the rooster was gone. Went for breaky with Jurgen and met a Danish guy who I had known in Xela. Bit of tele, then to the beach for a couple of hours where some of the Swedes were hanging out. A lovely Xmas dinner at Tranquilas, seeing Adeline and her friend, seems everyone eventually makes their way here. A Swiss guy called Lukas joined us, then the dive shop crowd rocked up, so that was Christmas afternoon sorted. I had a nice long conversation with a Swedish young lady called Sarah, and afterwards, she gave me a hug and said, "it was great talking to you, it's like having my dad on holiday with me." Not what I was hoping to hear! We all ended up back at Coco Loco to finish the night off.

Sounds like another cockerel has claimed the domain of the first one. Oh well, sort of used to it now. I put the tv on to more shocking news, a sense of dread engulfed me as I sat watching and listening about the unfolding horror in the Indian ocean as a tsunami was ripping across the waves, following a huge earthquake off the coast of Sumatra. I went for a walk, senses reeling from the terrible news. I bumped into Sarah, and she told me the party was called off that evening. A lot of Swedish families go to Thailand for Xmas and New year, and the Swedes in Utila at that time were all desperately calling home to find out if anyone they knew was there. Drifted towards Tranquilas for a couple and chat to others, my order for food was lost, so I had to put another one in, which meant having to drink another beer. Jurgen was sick, and was trying to see a doctor, which will probably put pay to his diving course. I couldn't help myself, so I watched the news for a bit, simply horrible, the death toll is going to be colossal. A quiet maudlin evening at Jade garden, which had interesting artistry displayed including in the toilet. On the way home, a couple of local guys spooked me, pretending they were going to rob me; wankers.

Jurgen was at the doctors for hours, but they don't seem to know what's wrong with him, but he's leaving as he can't dive with the illness. The news was bleak as expected, toll into the 100s of thousands, and many were missing. Go pay dive bill up to date, more than I thought. Bit of mailing, then finish The Long Silence of Mario Salviati, an okay book, a bit strange I suppose. Jurgen wanted to cook, he was definitely under the weather, but we ate and watched Grind, a film about skateboarders. I decided to pop out for a couple and saw Adeline and her friend, so glad I did.

I got up early to help Jurgen with his bags to the ferry, and said our goodbyes. Couldn't sleep again, so I had a major clean up and made breakfast. Laundry in, and get more electricity, then mail Henrik to inform him the room was available. I shouldn't have put the news on really because the continuing unfolding horror was upsetting. Lunch at my present local, then a boring arvo as it started to piss down. American cable is shit, the knowledge channels were all repeats, but found something on the History station, but the commercials drive you crazy. Out for a feed and beers at my local place, then an evening on the veranda with a little un and more bottles.

The day started okay, hummingbirds were busy around the feeders, the sun was out, and I made some eggs on toast for breaky. Then it deteriorated and the rains began, turning into downpours which became stair rods falling from the heavens. A diabolical deluge that went on for hours. I didn't want to see the news, knowing it would depress me, so read a book that I had acquired called The Life of Pi. In-between reading bouts, I got to thinking about the house back in the UK. Maybe it wouldn't be such a bad idea to sell up, and use the money for extensive travels, making my life less complicated; will see how things stand when I get back? Rain, rain and more damned rain. Go get log book stamps, the Swedes are out tonight, but need to be careful until I have other boarders. Food and beers later, then History channel, a programme about Bible codes caught my attention.

Still pissing down. Death toll now at 115,000, so sad. Another boring day, the weather hampers any outside activity. I'd given Henrik directions, and sat on the balcony to look out for him at the boat landing time. Then there he was, with his girlfriend Elsa, also Swedish, and they took the room. We had a catch up, Elsa was lovely and conversational. They were meeting up with the other Swedes at Jade garden, so I went along also. A pleasant evening, barracuda dinner, with a few coldies, and someone showed me seahorses living under the boardwalk.

The climate was much more agreeable, so got out for a stroll, the leg muscles were becoming soft. Other chores, avoiding the news, but everyone is talking about it, some of the Swedes knew casualties. It was New year's eve, so laid off drinking until later. Me, Henrik and Elsa met up with all the others where they were staying, then we went for a nice meal, and a dessert back at the girl's digs. Bundos for the rest of the night, and to Coco Loco to bring in 2005.

Midday when I surfaced from sleep. Tranquilas for a brunch, and hair of the dog. The afternoon on the beach with the Swedes, continuing to drink and smoke, pleasant start to the new year. Henrik asked if it was okay to invite everyone to ours? Yeah, why not, lets throw a party. Henrik and Elsa impressed me by knocking up a spaghetti dish for everybody, even though they had drunk and smoked all arvo. Some music playing, and an affable evening stretched out, companionable conversation, bit of singing and dancing, before I snuck off to bed at some point.

Long lie in again. The three of us got stuck into the clean up effort, drinking tea and snacking on what was leftover. I needed a workout, so suggested that we hike up the island. Similar day to last time, lots of small wildlife to observe, they were enamoured by the crabs, lizards, molluscs and birds that we saw, obviously nature lovers. Good feel factor of being out in the fresh air, with views and untamed creatures to survey. Legs adequately stretched, we returned to town, went to Bundos for a meal, meeting up with Adeline again, and settled in to watch The Life of Brian, for the umpteenth time for me, but it's so funny, I never seem to tire of it.

Casual morning, lovely having good companions to converse with, lively and interesting. Went to book dives for tomorrow, and lunch at Bundos. Henrik had decided to do his advanced course, so I helped him with some of the classroom stuff. Bit of a reading session, the book was enjoyable. A bon voyage evening, some of the Swedes are moving on. We were at Jade gardens, so I was lying down on the jetty watching the seahorses, quite rare to see them diving, so making the most of viewing the engrossing creatures in the wild. A round of goodbyes, and wandered back, needing to get to bed early to be fresh for the next day.

A bit of a windy morning, but you tend to forget about it when underwater. Great dive with Koos and his Russian girlfriend on Haliburton wreck. Interesting and eerie, two bicycles were chained to the hull, rusting away. The story went that there was a bit of an arsehole here a while back, and he peddled around, pissing everybody off, an abrupt and rude sort of character. So they nicked his bike and chained it to the vessel at the site. No one knew where the other bike had come from? We also saw two huge barracudas, cleaner shrimp and French angelfish. Read back at the house, then Elsa was home, so more chat with her. Soup lunch at my local, and a quiet afternoon watching a movie. There had been some dengue fever cases, so everyone was paranoid about getting bitten by mosquitoes that carry the disease. Daniel, Henrik's mate, had been one of the victims, but had recovered. He came round for the evening and Henrik knocked up food for us all. Couple more films and a few beers plus a toke on the veranda made for a pleasurable night.

H and E invited me to join them at a cay for the day. We made a packed lunch, and hired some snorkel gear, then went to find a pirogue skipper to negotiate with to take us to Water cay. Lovely few hours on an idyllic beach of light coloured sand, with palm trees and coconut groves, and turquoise shallow Caribbean sea.

There were reefs offshore, but some were difficult to get to because of current, but saw an array of fish including cowfish. We watched the numerous pelicans diving from the air to catch their fodder, gulping down the catch as they sat on the surface. Got a bit burnt sitting chatting with a doobie, and snacking on our filled rolls, crisps, drinking just water to stay hydrated. The guy came to collect us about 3pm, dropping us back at the jetty. Home for a bit of a lie down, before going to Dave's for dinner.

Repeating dive sites now, so two on Spotted bay and Labyrinth. I couldn't find a wetsuit that fitted me, so went without, but dropped too much weight to compensate for reduced buoyancy. My mask was filling slowly, so had to keep clearing it. Most interesting thing on the first was two porcupine fish performing some sort of mating ritual. Drumfish, lobster, cleaner shrimp on the second, but a distinct lack of activity, not even seeing stations with cleaner wrasse! The night dive was called off, so ended up at Tranquilas for a few and something to eat with Henrik, Elsa and

Daniel. On the way home, there were some kids having a mango fight, we picked a few up to take home. Someone had left a near full bottle of Bacardi on our stoep.

I got up to go dive Black hills, but it was also cancelled, it's quite a way and they need more people to cover costs. Tried to go back to sleep, but no joy, so I caught up with the diary and news on tv. I had to get a visa extension, so went to sort that out, quite shocked at how much it cost. Fried chicken lunch, and a catch up with email. Watched a film, and read a while, then Henrik was back, and we got ready for our night dive on Ron's wreck, guided by Willy John. Lots of crustaceans covering the small vessel, and bioluminescence when you waved your hand through the water. Sting rays, and squid and some luminant fish, nice corals established firmly all over. We started on the Bacardi when we got home, then went for a few at a bar, having a feed there also. H and E had their lobster dinner that they were craving. At Coco Loco's, we sat on the jetty and saw quite a few shooting stars. A guy sold us a spliff, and the evening morphed into that combination of drink and drugs, a sort of sinking sensation. I took them to The Bar in the Bush, rough as fuck there, but we were pretty pissed and stoned, so oblivious to it.

Not much doing that day. Read and tv, and got the Spanish learning material out again, trying to brush up, not having had a convo en español for a while, and heading back to the mainland soon. Sometimes you would go into a shop and the staff would be talking in a strange tongue, which was the local creole, then revert back to perfect English to serve you. Elsa didn't speak much Spanish, so those two conversed in Swedish or English. Henrik seemed to have Spanish firmly embedded in his head, and helped me a bit, chatting, but with little enthusiasm. I was a little worried at how fast it disappeared without being practised. A movie, they cooked, and I washed up. We sat on the balcony finishing off the Bacardi, still not knowing who had left it there. We decided to go to Coco Loco for a couple, but it ended up as a big night as lots of people partied, drinking, and dancing until 3am.

Already the afternoon when I got up. Lunch at the local, and sit inside reading, the guys have gone to the beach. Couple at Tranquilas with a meal, and meet H & E in Bundos for the pub quiz. Willy John joined us as the fourth member of our team, and we stormed it again. A great geography question, where you had to identify many countries from just a map outline, which we got high scores for. A few take outs to return home with, asking people for weed, but no luck scoring any. Still, a lovely evening, chatting and drinking, marvellous company in them two.

They overslept and missed the early ferry. A casual late morning meal and plenty of tea, talk was easy and interesting. We might cross paths again somewhere, so would continue to keep in touch by email. It was sad seeing them off on the 2pm departure, it had been nice and a lot of fun having them there. Booked diving for tomorrow, and queued to get cash from the bank, need an ATM to be installed really! Wanted to use up some of the food left, so cooked indoors, I hate waste, having seen some of the poorer parts of our planet, it just seems incredibly immoral to throw away any consumable produce. Finished Life of Pi, then watched Devil's Advocate starring Keanu Reeves and Al Pacino.

Did my 200th dive with Willy John, James, a local dive guide, a Welsh guy and a Swedish chap. Lots of good and unusual hard and soft corals, all in good health. A green moray, lots of cleaner shrimp under a ledge, two porcupinefish, and a potato grouper. Filefish in soft plant like coral, yellow cleaner wrasse, spotted lobsters and 100s of tiny crabs in the corals. A plethora of reef fish, they are returning from their breeding grounds apparently, such an array of colour with dappling sunlight, sometimes diving seems very dream-like. Henrik had given me a dive he had paid for and couldn't do, so was trying to organise that with Neil, but he said it wasn't transferable, so gave me a tee shirt instead. Pupusas for lunch, and went to the book exchange at Bundos, then phoned Ally, having a good catch up and she might be coming for a visit wherever I am in March. Got my hair cut, but her scissors and trimmer needed sharpening, so a bit painful. Trying to get a bit of grass for later, but seems dry everywhere, a bust happened by all accounts. A chicken and mashed potato feed, then to the cinema to watch Collateral, which I didn't particularly enjoy. Coco Loco for a couple, still no go with weed, and a lot of folk have left, so it's looking like time to move on.

Lie in, use up the last of the food listening to tv news. Start to organise for onwards travel, packing up and paying dues at the dive shop. Long mail from Maike, will have to ponder a response. Sopa de pollo lunch at my local cafe, collect laundry and finish packing. Watch Matchstick Men with Nicolas Cage which was okay. Tranquillas for a beer, then to another place to eat, and re meet Ab and Minnka who's paths crossed with mine in El Salvador, so spent the evening with them, showing them the house later as they might take it on after I've moved out tomorrow. The new annoyance whilst trying to sleep was a barking dog somewhere nearby.

Up at 5am, and final sorting out, before heading for the jetty one last time with all my belongings. A 6.20am crossing back to La Ceiba, up top to see the views around, the hills over the coastline of mainland Honduras look verdant and intact, no deforestation visible. A bee was keeping up with the boat, all the way, zooming ahead, then dropping back, to catch up again, a feat of endurance for such a small organism. It could have landed and rested any time it felt like it, but seemed like it was determined on a good workout; Superbee maybe. Bags were searched, looking for drugs I presume, the war on recreationals just appeared to be ludicrous, all that money spent to stop people enjoying a bit of herb. Shared a taxi to town with two girls and a guy going to San Pedro, one of the girls gave me a banana to eat. Farted and faffed, waiting for the departure of a chicken bus to Tocoa, dozed for most of the ride. Had to change there, and a much slower one to Trujillo, which we reached about 2pm. A kilometre walk to town, and checked into the Mar de Plata hotel, hot and sweating, it was a very warm and humid day.

After a bite to eat, I attempted to book onto a tour of La Mosquitia, but I had no joy at all, and was told that it is completely the wrong time of year, and the whole area is more or less under water, normal during the height of the wet season. Really pays to do your research to avoid disappointments like that one. There were no other tourists, obviously everyone else had looked into it better than me, and I was actively discouraged from pursuing the endeavour further. A lovely cold shower back in the room, and up on the rooftop terrace for smashing views over the Caribbean and inland mountain range. Out to eat at Rincón de los Amigos for pizza and three beers, sitting at a bench on the beach with only a cat for company. At least I'm starting to use my Spanish again, and relieved that it all comes back again as you begin to exercise it.

Jamón, huevos, frijoles y tortillas para el desayuno. Need to get some more tea bags, no one seems to have heard of regular black tea. Check one final place for tours, but it ain't gonna happen. It was a pleasant day, a bit windy, but decided to walk along the beach to Santa Fe Garifuna village. Quite a way, a fair few kilometres, the sand soft in places, the tide was in, and driftwood hampered the progress, having to navigate through piles of the stuff. The regular gusts whipped up the particles, blasting them into your face, but mostly had the whole coastline to myself. A dead horse in the surf at one point. A decent workout by the time I arrived in Santa Fe, populated by people of African descent, their ancestors would have arrived on the awful slave ships, brought by the Spanish colonists.

The local Creole was unintelligible to me, but some folk spoke Spanish and even a little English. A very interesting little settlement of mostly bamboo, cane and wicker built dwellings, though there were some block structures also. Fishing boats, like dug out canoes, lined the beaches, chickens pecked around, and simple agriculture was practised, so with the plenty of the seas, and streams coming from the hills, bringing fresh water, it all looked reasonably self sufficient. I guess some produce also comes from town. I sat and ate a traditional meal of fried fish, banana bread and plantain in coconut soup, and a blessed glass of iced tea. A white guy spotted me and sat down to chat, he was from New York, and had come here to retire. I didn't think I had the energy to return on foot, so hitched a lift on the road with a truck driven by a couple who worked for The European Union disaster relief effort. Others were picked up along the way, and a bumpy, slow drive back on a heavily potholed route, kids waving as we went by, like in Africa. Could have guessed I was in Africa, if I was placed there blindfolded. Went back to the same as last night for dinner, the cat scrounging food again. Suddenly, the heavens opened, and I got under cover, and had to wait for a break in the downpour before legging it back to the digs.

It rained like bejesus all through the night, and all the next morning. The lane outside was a river, and even with a brolly, to go out would result in a drenching. By 10am, it was still raining like a bastard, so I resigned to staying put and paid for another night at the hotel. It was going to be a long and boring day. I was right. Later, much later, after what seemed like an eternity, I borrowed an umbrella, and went to get something to eat, wearing my shorts and sandals as the roads were torrents of water, and a lake had formed at the bottom of the street. Watched some wildlife documentary in Spanish, read, and smoked too many fags. CNN en Español, the commentary difficult to keep up with, they speak far too fast. A phrase used a lot by me was "habla más despacio por favor." Meaning please speak more slowly. Boredom, boredom, boredom. I borrowed the brolly again, and went to a place nearby, and sat with a couple of coldies and a pork chop feed, listening to Total Eclipse of the Heart playing over and over for some reason!

Woke up at 6am, it was still raining but eased somewhat from yesterday. The electricity was off, but got ready to leave in the half light. A timely break in the precipitation allowed me to get to the bus terminal, where I got on the one back to Tocoa. There was a chicken bus leaving for Juticalpa at 9.30am, and was told it went via La Unión, so I bought a ticket and sat for a meal and tea in a pleasant little comedor. I didn't realise that we were doubling back on ourselves, the whole landscape was flooded, a big brown lake, with trees growing out of it, and the sky was overcast, so not aware of the direction of travel. When we eventually arrived in a town called San Esteban, I consulted the map, to discover that we had traversed a completely different route, and I wouldn't be getting to La Unión that day. It became one of those endless road syndrome periods, the tarmac was patchy, quite a lot of submerged track, that we bumped and bounced along. Uphill climbs and downhill crawls, the vistas hilly, and a lot more evident deforestation, quite agriculture intensive, with plenty of cattle, including many brahman.

A few stops for a smoke, then there was some improvement in the highway, and we accomplished some heads of speed occasionally. Very rural villages, some looking quite poor, back into the developing world again now. Suddenly, we arrived at a junction, and turned onto a main road that was properly surfaced, and shortly into Juticalpa, now 5.30pm. Checked into El Paso, a nice guest house, with en suite rooms, tv, CNN in English. A shit, shave and a shower, before going out to look around, the usual imposing white cathedral, central to everything. Lots of internet cafes, that seem to be springing up everywhere now. There was a Chinese restaurant in the plaza, so a couple of beers, and chow mein Honduras style. More beggars than previously seen, poverty was increasing the further south I went through Central America. Spent the rest of the evening watching Animal Planet en Español.

Leisurely morning. To the plaza to find breaky, and stop to check mail on the way back, but the speed of the connection convinced me to give it up. At the station, there weren't many buses, and queues of people, so walked to the road, and hailed one heading west. I jumped down in Limones, the road was fine, so it didn't take long. Several hours of waiting for one going to La Unión, then a windy dirt track and a climb back up to over 1000 metres. Pine forest landscapes, but plenty of trucks loaded with trunks heading back down, so the usual story of extensive cutting was underway. Finally we pulled into the dusty blackwater of LU, a French guy had been sitting further forward than me, and we went to the hotel Karol together, chatting away, my Spanish was getting better again. Tried to gather info about visiting the National park, but everything was already closed for the day. Too many street dogs, never understand why nothing is ever done about them in these countries, they live a miserable life, and a bit of neutering would eliminate the problem, can't be that expensive to undertake. Some food at a shop by the plaza, no bars, so buy a couple from the store to take back.

No water from the faucet! The bananas I bought were hard and unpleasant. I went to try and register for the NP, but was told I could just go, there was no charge. Walked along the trail, hoping for a lift, but nothing came past me all day, just a pick up going in the opposite direction. Alpine forest, and great views over the mountain range from time to time, but no one else did I see, which was pleasant and peaceful, some birdsong the only sounds that reached my ears. It was 14 kilometres to the park entrance, and I hiked about 7 before deciding that I would have to turn back, my legs were aching as it was mostly uphill. Started to encounter folk as I got back nearer to the town, and felt like I'd had an adequate keep fit session. There were a bunch of kids at the hotel, so I practised my Spanish with them, showing them my maps. Tried to get fags, but my brand unavailable, so had to buy stronger ones, or give up? Nah, not an option. It was a one horse settlement, but was liking being away from civilization for a spell. At the comedor, the only meal that they could knock up was the ubiquitous pollo frito con arroz, frijoles y tortillas. Another early night followed.

Car alarms being set off during the night disturbed my sleep, but got a few hours, and up at 6am; I had to knock up someone to let me out. The bus wasn't quite ready, the driver still in the process of waking. Back to Limones, felt hungry, but will just wait until I get to Tegucigalpa before eating. A big bus, like a coach came along heading for the capital, but no seats, so had to stand for a spell. Someone got down at one stop, and the bus guy collared me a seat next to a bit of a nutter. He raved on in Spanish, I was not able to follow some of his speech, but I did my best. He then reeled off the capital cities of all the European countries, quite impressive. He entertained and amused me for the ride anyway, a nice madman. Numerous sets of roadworks coming into the city, and a conglomerate of crudely built houses up and over the surrounding hills, looked to me like a disaster in waiting. A taxi to my choice of hostel, but it was full, so went to The Tobacco Inn, which had dorm beds available, and only me in the room where I was allocated a bed.

Needed food, so got a Wendy's burger and chips, American fast food outlets are in all the bigger centres. Typical busy developing world capital city, polluted air, chaos on the streets, blaring horns, and a million people trying to eke out an existence. Not the best examples of architecture I've seen in The Americas, the central plaza could have been pretty, but appeared tired, and was weather and soot stained, the cathedral in dire need of a paint job. An hour online, constantly trying to keep up with mail. I met Kristy, an American woman, back at the digs, and she might come to La Tigra tomorrow with me. Bit of shopping for supplies to take with us, and, after a shower, to the bar. I got talking to Tom, the owner of the establishment, also an American. An education in wokeness, the original meaning of the word, to have a keener understanding of how our world works, The Deep State and all that. He had become seriously disillusioned with how The USA had unfolded politically in recent years, and left to set up this business in Tegucigalpa. He especially ranted about Bush's foreign policies. A Mexican band played soft background music. I shared a chinky with an Irish chap called Michael, and there was an annoying Israeli also present, just generally being arrogant. Few more beers, bit pissed, then turn in. The dorm had filled up during the course of the day.

Got up at 6am, ablutions, and boiled egg, banana and tea breakfast. Wasn't sure if Kristy was going to come, but she suddenly appeared, keen to get some nature and exercise. We walked to the bus stand, and embarked on an hour long ride to Jutiapa, then a steep uphill hike to the visitor centre. Ten dollars entrance fee, and we started out for a climb into the National park La Tigra, which is a beautifully preserved cloud forest: at an altitude of over 2000 metres, you are shrouded in the mist most of the time. It was a lush tropical jungle, many species fully adapted to the moist environment, full of old growth trees, bromeliads everywhere, mosses, ferns and fungi galore; a very special reserve.

Didn't see so much wildlife, as expected, but a few bird species, unfortunately not a quetzal, which I was eager to sight. Sendero cascada, for a short food break, gazing at the amazing waterfall displayed for our pleasure, a sight to behold. We continued onto El Rosario, the going quite tough at times, some boardwalks in place over more difficult spots. Then we exited the park, and a downhill trek to San Juancito, my legs by now killing me, a thoroughly decent workout.

We met José and another American chap, who told us about a guided tour of the metal and paper factory, or cultural centre, which Kristy was enthusiastic to visit. A pleasant hour or so there, quite interesting, Kristy's Spanish was near fluent, and I got something out of it, a rest for my aching limbs. It was two kilometres to the main road, but luckily got a lift in a pick up truck, where we caught a bus back to Tegucigalpa. A second to the city centre, and a short walk to the hostel, good day, Kristy was excellent company. There was a message from a peace corp guy who she fancied, and was in a flap, even blaming me for inviting her to go to La Tigra, resulting in her missing the call! No one twisted your arm love. Spell in the net cafe, and sort bags ready for tomorrow. Out to eat, and go see the cathedral lit up in purple lighting, looks better like that, the black stains less visible. Sample one in the bar, chat more to Tom, a really switched on guy, and he told me stuff that has stuck with me over the years. Things that I already had suspicions about were sort of confirmed, a few hundred very wealthy elites, decide global policy by lobbying governments around the world (giving them money in roundabout ways) to keep a sort of status quo. Us that are born in Western countries, are mostly okay, we can have reasonably nice lives, but billions in developing states? Why are all those nations always still in the process of advancement, but never quite make a breakthrough? Corrupt authorities? The charities and aid agencies always need more money? Someone, somewhere seems to benefit from keeping them down?

The lady who came in to prepare the included breakfast was usually late, but I wanted to have my toast and tea, so waited, stashing a pack in the storage facility. Ended up walking all the way to the stand for San Pedro buses, markets being set up along the pavements. It was three quarters full, so I bought a ticket, found a seat at the back, and we were shortly away, escaping the clutches of the city. Nice scenic drive, mountains in the distance, and tropical vegetation, forest with a smattering of farmland. Ascents and descents over troublesome hills, and a long straight down a valley, crossing rivers, plenty of water in the landscape. Fell asleep for a spell, dorm syndrome last night left me short of shut eye. Then into Pito Solo, and spotted the hotel Los Remos, my intended accommodation, so grabbed my bag and shouted for the driver to pull over, fighting my way down the bus. A nice room for 150 lempira, right on the shore of Lago Yojoa, with great views over the body of water and a range of hills to the east. Quick walk around the village, then explore the grounds of the hotel, and gaze out across the lake. Zopilotes, or buzzards, scavenging through the vegetable scraps, flowering trees and shrubs made for a gratifying scene. Short siesta, shower and read for a bit, then to an eatery I'd clocked earlier for a couple and a tilapia feed. There were bats feeding on the bugs that were attracted to the dim lighting outside of the room.

Easy morning enjoying my surroundings. To town to get fodder, and fill my bottles from a dispenser of purified water. Go get photos of the zopilotes that I wanted, and catch the local bus to La Guama, along the shoreline. Then another to Peña Blanca, through rural countryside, and endless lake views. A stroll around the sweet little town, before the last ride to San Buenaventura, for the brief trek to Cascada Pulhapanzak, another one of those astounding marvels of the natural world that most people have never heard of, until you are in its vicinity. A long while gawking, and listening to the roar of the bellowing H2O, before being disturbed by a girl. She was local, so got chatting, and did some of the short trails to the bottom, getting soaked by the spray, but lovely to share it with someone else.

My legs were still hurting from the tough hike the day before yesterday, but a gentle amble back, and the same in return to Pito

Solo. Feeling satiated, a great natural beauty day, I fell asleep back at the digs. Later, a shower, a bit of a read, and write up the journal, before heading to town, for a meal. Ordered, sipping a coldie, and chatting with a taxi driver, but a long while passed, before I made enquiries. They'd forgotten, and didn't seem bothered about serving me, so I went down the road where I'd eaten breaky. Another beer, and they asked if I wanted chilli cooked into my food, and were amused that I enthusiastically accepted the addition to my dinner. It came quickly, but fancied one more bevvie, which I drank casually. Returning to the hotel was a bit dodgy, as no street lights, trucks and bikes zooming by, made it a tad scary. The gate was locked again, but the security guard let me in. Sat watching the bats, before retiring.

I'd ordered breakfast at the hotel, so had another lovely relaxed morning, sitting in the grounds, and eating, drinking my tea, taking in the tranquil setting that I was privy to. Out on the road by 10am, and soon enough, a chicken bus heading my way, terminating in Siguatepeque. A big bus was leaving imminently, a bit more expensive, but better to get moving. I'm becoming complacent with the magnitude of attractiveness, constantly bombarding my vision, Central America is overflowing with such ravishing vistas; and I'd seen it all on the way up. Into the city, housing built all around the hillsides as mentioned before, it's ugly, you really feel for the people who live there, crime rife, and a daily grind for survival. Decided to walk back, and found no one in when I knocked on the door. Spent an hour in the net cafe, then tried again. Still no answer, and Tom has gone out on his bike apparently. Eventually, about 4pm, Tom turned up, so I got a bed back in the empty dorm. Absolutely no other guests, so chat with Tom, telling him I'm going to Nicaragua tomorrow. He told me there is a $7 entry fee which I didn't know about, and had been frugal in recent days, so as not to have to draw more cash in Honduras. That was out the window now, so I went to hit the ATM, then a feed. Three Finnish girls had arrived, but kept to themselves. A quiet evening, just a couple in the hostel bar, Tom didn't seem very communicative that night.

Bit of chat with the girls, one is really tidy, not a hope in hell for me. Tea and toast, pay my dues, and goodbyes to Tom, learnt a lot from him, plenty more food for thought to mull over. Couldn't find a colectivo, so had to get a taxi to the terminal, and straight onto a transport for Danli. More joyous scenery to gape at, my neural networks are saturated with such visions of wonder. A fast undeviating drive to El Paraiso, then a smaller bus to the border town of Las Manos. Another little unknown fee of $3 to exit Honduras, changed my lempira into Nicaraguan córdobas, not far off one to one, about 30 córdobas to £1; also got a US $10 note for the entry fee into Nicaragua. A lady filled in the embarkation form for me, and I got quizzed by customs, dodgy looking fucker that I am. It was going to be a day on buses, which I don't actually mind most of the time, especially if the roads are in good nick. So a first to Ocotal, then a second to Esteli, where I decided that was enough, being about 4pm by then.

Checked into the hotel Miraflores, no water till 6pm, Nicaragua was a degree more third world than even Honduras I was starting to discover. Got a decent meat feed, kebabs and chicken, with all the trimmings, at a cafe with outside plastic tables and chairs. Kids and dogs competed with each other in the begging game, such poverty right in your face all around. Señora got the whip out to the dogs, who ran off yelping, in anticipation of pain. I gave coins to some teenage boys, then three younger lads were staring longingly at my food, right in front of me. The lady was going to shoo them away, but I stopped her, and ate a bit more before pushing the plate across to them. They looked at each other in astonishment! Then they divided the leftovers between them with dignity, obviously taking care of each other, and the oldest made sure the youngest got his fair share. Nothing was left on the plate, and they thanked me profusely, it was one of those happy and sad events that has stuck with me. Of course, you can't feed everyone, that's the job of parents and The State in some cases, but I was wondering what was wrong within the country that had led to so much hardship. Nice hot shower when the water finally came on, then a couple at the hotel bar. Slept in my clothes as not sure of the cleanliness of the bed sheets.

A nice cafe down the road served me a desayuno típico, which is eggs, beans, fried plantain and tortillas, washed down with tea. A shortish walk, so travelled light, just drinking water. South on the pan American highway, and found the back road to the falls. I stopped to converse with a guy standing on a bridge, who looked indigenous, and I couldn't really understand what he was saying, so assumed he was talking a native language. Not many other people about, and a 5 to 6 kilometre hike to Cascada Salto de Estanzuela, not the most impressive I've seen, but a pleasant trek through some natural habitat, a small laguna under the cataract. Sat watching the butterflies, dragonflies and lizards for a while, a smattering of birds, too fleeting to identify. Heading back, a young boy charged me 10 córdobas for walking on his father's land. I got offered a lift, I think, I'm not understanding what people are saying? Anyway, I was enjoying the exercise, so I declined. Cows were coming up to the fence line to stare at me, maybe thinking I was a predator?

Back in town, I sat with a soda, and bought the second ciggie of the day, trying once again to cut down, you could purchase single sticks. Bit of mailing, one from Rob, saying Jenny's mother had died. I was keen to volunteer for a turtle conservation program, but it seemed like I was there at the wrong time of year for egg laying. Read and relaxed for a couple of hours, then went for the first and a feed at another eatery in town. A man was trying to scrounge a fag, and the women proprietor chased him off, cracking her whip, much to the amusement of the street kids. She kept a vigil with her lash fending off the dogs and children, but I couldn't help giving some coins to some of them, though it seemed like taking a piss off a pier, literally a drop in the ocean. A clear night and a full moon to observe, sat outside the hotel bar sipping a couple. Watched some baseball, which is Nicaragua's national sport.

At the cafe, two Yanks were talking animatedly about the cubic capacity of their rucksacks, don't think I will get in on that conversation. Check out, a taxi to the bus station, and a short ride to

San Isidro, the landscape had become distinctly drier looking. It is a very diverse country weather wise, and I'd crossed a climatic divide maybe? Or was it because I was in the vicinity of the Pacific ocean which has different patterns to the Caribbean side? Anyway, it was the dry season, and with it, the scenery had a parched dusty look about it. Got dropped at the T junction where there was a police checkpoint, the cops friendly whilst they inspected my passport. Bus to León, starting to see volcanoes again, including a perfect cone shaped one, which was Momotombo. Chat to an American girl who had hiked a volcano for the full moon last night.

Hostel La Clinica sounded nice, so got a taxi there, and it was lovely, really friendly lady hosts, though quite a bit of building work was underway. They explained why I was having language trouble. Nicaragua has a lot of local dialects in its Spanish, some call it Nicañol. A sort of lazy style of speaking, words shortened or endings not included, and fast, so I was using the phrase "habla más despacio por favor" a lot. The women just fell into doing that for me anyway, and they corrected me often, which I wasn't sure was a good thing; fine for here, but what about when I leave the country? Oh, why does it have to be so confusing? Visited the ATM, bought some sandals, and looked around the engaging city, finding somewhere to fill my water bottle. A lady called Maria sat to talk with me, and I chatted away, her telling me about León. Then, inevitably in Nicaragua, the heart sob story comes out, deaf and dumb kids in that instance. I gave her 50 córdobas, you can't speak to anyone without having to part with some cash. Had mail from Henrik and Elsa, they were in León, so go find their place, and catch up. Another Swedish guy and a Canadian called Geoff were also there, and a joint was on the burn. We ended up on a session, drinking, laughing and playing pool in a local bar. Had difficulty finding my way home.

Bit hungover, I didn't get round to eating anything last night, so really hungry. Went to find a cafe for breaky, and back to collect my beach stuff. The ladies wanted me to buy some fresh fish to bring back. Had trouble finding the bus, people seemed to be giving me contradictory directions, sending me back and forth. Eventually locate it and shortly away for the brisk drive to Poneloya. A lovely beach, hardly any other people, the men are drinking already, maybe something to do with celebrating the baseball game last night? Walk up and down the stretch of sand, flocks of pelicans fishing and flying in formation. Got a bit of a brown off, reading a book, then went for a feed, chatting to the man in the restaurant. Pretty much the only meat available was chicken, so chicken it is then. A few minutes later, there was a commotion outside, sounded like panicking hens, maybe a dog was bothering them? Then the same guy walked back in with a live bird under his arm, my lunch I suspected: well, you don't get fresher than that.

A longer hike along the coastline, with a nature reserve to my left; lots more pelicans and herons were sighted. Back in town, I asked around for fish to buy, and got two reasonably large specimens that were surprisingly cheap. A glorious sunset on the return journey to León, and a taxi back to the hostel, where the family was already eating. So they put the fish in the freezer, and I went to Via Via for dinner. Tried to find Henrik and Elsa, but they were out, so I ambled around taking in the fine architecture of that beautiful city, the lighting perfectly complimented all the colours. Went back to Via Via for a nightcap, and H and E were there, with Daniel, so had a couple and chatted with them.

The fish was thawing out, and it was decided to have it for breakfast, so had to wait until it was ready, starting to rue getting involved with the venture. Went for a juice down the road whilst waiting, and preparations were underway on my return. Really nice pescado morning meal, so the regrets receded. A long walk to the bus station, and the La Paz transport was leaving, so got going straight away. Another to Puerto Momotombo, a thoroughly scenic drive with volcanoes dotted about all around. Strolled to the shore of Lago Xolotlán, and just soaked in the stupendous view of the perfect cone shaped fully active outlet of magma.

I stared for a long time, lost in thought about the powers of Mother Nature. A juvenile dog started following me about, wagging its tail in excitement, but I didn't encourage it too much, as there was no way I could adopt it. Maria touted me for the guided tour of Ruinas de León viejo, a settlement that had been buried under ash over time, but the residents had already moved, knowing that it was a precarious location. An engaging couple of hours in pleasant company. After returning to León, I showered, went to eat, and saw Daniel. There was live music playing, so we settled in for a session, meeting a lot of the locals, and ended up arseholed.

A quiet day, nursing a hangover, the ladies ribbed me about coming in late last night, they reckoned that I had a woman on the go. Already lunch time, I went for a chinky feed, drinking lots of tea, and juice, which was available everywhere. Few chores such as catching up on mail, phoned Ally but only got the machine. A lazy arvo reading, then back to the plaza with Andreas who was staying at the casa also. He was studying world politics, so quite interesting to talk to. Couple of beers, not going down well that evening, and settled for hot dogs and chips for supper. A steady two or three more, there was a power cut, so candles were dished out, and a girl borrowed ours for a while, then bought us a drink in thanks! Back to sleep early.

Up at the crack of dawn, and go to Via Via for food, the only place open that time of day. Goodbyes to my fabulous lady hosts, it was great there, a really pleasant guest house, and the women were friendly and funny. A taxi to the bus station to board the Managua bound transport, Nicaragua's capital city, another one that could easily be skipped, with little of interest for tourists. To the colectivo point, and ride the one heading for Masaya, a short distance away. Trouble finding the hotel Regis as few of the streets have name signs, but get there eventually after asking directions. An agreeable little hostel, the town seemed full of craft shops, arts and trinkets for sale everywhere. Spoke to Ally, and she is definitely still coming, most likely to Costa Rica. Bit of lunch from the stalls along the pavements, always a good and cheap way to nourish yourself. A walk to Lago Masaya shore, but the steep banks opposite are the borough's rubbish dump, and the lake is polluted apparently. Back through a poorer part of town, shit and trash everywhere, not impressed, some basic sanitation facilities need installing. Few hygiene chores, then a feed and a couple next door, before a quiet evening after several hectic ones.

The hotel breakfast was good and healthy, fruit and juice, bread, rice, beans and eggs, an excellent starter for the day's activities. A hike up to the top of town and along the highway to an old fort, which had some interesting history, but the views were more impressive to me. Another crowd in a pick up truck, who I saw regularly as the day went by, and chatted to a runner who had stopped for a breather. Caught a bus to the entrance of National park volcán Masaya, paid my fee, and walked to the visitor centre. A lot of information about our planet's volcanic activity, scary stuff, but one of the reasons why our species evolved, just the right amount of dynamism. Also heaps about the park's flora and fauna which I hoped to see some of, but the usual environmental problems caused by human industry. The hike to the crater rim was mostly flat, but the last kilometre was uphill, so it got very hot and sweaty. A guide was stalking me, having declined his services, he was waiting for an opportunity to pounce when I suddenly couldn't read my guide book anymore. Lava flows, and flowering trees galore, the soil is super rich and lots of sulphurous smelling steam. Glimpses of high temperature magma down inside the caldera, when the veil lifted occasionally, and amazingly, green parakeets living around the interior of the basin! They are chocoyos, a native Nicaraguan variety, which might be a seperate species. I met a couple of women who were from Scotland and Newcastle; they were fun, typical Geordie humour, a bit dirty. We headed back to town together, hitching a lift in the end. Met up with them for dinner in a place with a nice courtyard.

Couldn't resist another morning meal like yesterday, only 25 córdobas, a bargain. Visited the internet cafe so I could refill my water bottle, but sent a quick couple of mails anyway. Checked out and walked east, eventually intersecting the highway. A small bus to the road for Laguna de Apoyo, only seven kilometres, and began to saunter along; luckily another minibus happened by and picked me up, turned out to be quite far. Struggling with conversation again, Nicaraguan Spanish really was difficult for me to understand fully. Checked into the guest house attached to proyecto ecológico, and enquired about diving, but they don't accept visa, and not enough cash on me, and certainly no ATMs in that remote location. A stroll around the lakeside reassured me that I wasn't really missing anything, lots of trash up the banks, and in the water, oil slicks were visible also. Naively thought that I was coming to a pristine environment, but, the human presence, along with farming, including many pigs and chickens being raised, and introduced fish species for sapien consumption, told me a different story. I sat at a beach bar for a beer, and enjoyed the sunset, bats feeding on the insects, many stray and mangy dogs about. Nearer home, I had a feed plus another beer, and went back for a quiet evening. Dogs barking through the night made sleep challenging, and a bat was suddenly flying around my room. It gave me a good insight into how brilliant a bat's echolocation was, it never hit anything, nor came close to me. I opened the door, and it left immediately on sensing the change, even though it was pitch dark. When things settled down eventually, I had a tranquil sleep, lulled by the gentle sound of water lapping at the shoreline.

Breakfast was included, so I took advantage of that, chatting to a group of German guys also staying there. I shared a taxi with some others to the main road, and flagged down the Granada bound chicken bus, just C10 to get there, not very far at all. I'd saved on not diving, so decided on a more expensive hostel, The Oasis, very nice, with a swimming pool in the grounds. Free internet also, so caught up on chores online, mostly mail. Watched a BBC World service bulletin on the tv in the lobby, lush, so much luxury. A good look around the other main city of Nicaragua, but it's very similar to León, maybe I was becoming complacent with all the fine architecture of the region. There were horse drawn carriage rides, but I didn't really want to support that, the nags looked tired, it was hot in the daytime. A volcano to climb nearby, but I'm going to Ometepe next, which has two, so also decided to skip that, had my fair share of them recently. I visited the old railway station, which was a museum of sorts for steam trains. They need to do something about the waste, so much trash in the river made it ugly, it could be so pretty without all that garbage spoiling the views. Back for a dip in the pool, then time for the first of the day, got talking to a lady from Denver. Back out to eat at a place I spied earlier, which turned out to be a good choice. A big crowd around the plaza, and music from large speakers, so sat for a nightcap there soaking in the fiesta ambiance.

Great having free internet, can get loads done, so fully up together with mail. No rush today, so relax and read for a spell, such a calm, unhurried atmosphere permeated through the building; thought about staying put an extra night, but decided to move in the end. To the stand for buses to Rivas, about 60 to 70 kilometres, and start to see the twin volcanic cones of Isla de Ometepe. Asia style touts for share taxis to San Jorge, so take one with a local guy called Roger, who could speak passable English, giving me a break from trying to comprehend what people were saying in Spanish. A rough crossing on a ropey old boat to Moyogalpa, Roger told me he could guide me around tomorrow, so I made an arrangement with him. Gulls shadowed the vessel, in hope of food scraps maybe? A lone fisherman in a small craft; the cone shaped peaks looming larger, as we inch towards the landmass. Finally, we parked up at the jetty, and Roger helped me to the Hotelito Aly, with decent rooms con baño privado, and nice settings. Will stay a few days here and chill. A spot of bother with the lock on the door, which the handyman fixed promptly. A look around, herons and egrets, and a scale model of the island, which was fascinating for me, love such things. Sit and eat, sipping a coldie with an older Austrian guy, who turned out to be a bit of an opinionated buffoon. The power went off, so had one more by candlelight, and luckily had brought my torch to find my way back.

Pretty average breakfast here, have been spoilt recently with all the excellent ones. Roger no show, so jump on a bus for Altagracia, which goes around the southern route, anti clockwise. Through quite a few small rural settlements, Volcán Concepción features large to my left, a real beauty, at over 1600 metres, and blows every few years, so extremely active. Quite thrilling to be in the vicinity of such natural power. Agriculture in abundance, bananas and maize mostly, the soils are rich in nutrients. Very scenic little place, peaceful and calm; tranquilla. Altagracia is a small municipality, with a central plaza, took me all of five minutes to look around, though the typical painted buildings of coordinated colour that is consistent through Central America. Started to walk in the direction of San Marcos, to complete the circumnavigation of the western lump of Ometepe. A dirt road now, people calling out hola and adios. A bus pottered along, so jumped on to SM, but nothing really there but a smattering of dwellings. Don't think many tourists come here, as the kids were now staring in awe at the alien, and when I attempted to chat, all I got in reply was shy giggles.

A pear juice refreshment, then just continued to hike back to Moyogalpa, about 5 or 6 kilometres. Birds a plenty including blue magpies; lizards scurrying across my pathway. Cattle being herded, free range chickens and pigs profuse. Young boys racing horses looked quite dangerous, but they were obviously experienced riders. La Flor and La Concepción were the two villages I passed through, more curiosity from the locals, lots of hellos and waving. It was hot, dry and dusty, my hip seemed to be playing up, I hoped that I hadn't inherited my dad's skeleton problems. The views were stupendous, the volcano constantly drawing my eyes, and the blue waters of Lago de Nicaragua or Cocibolca, a freshwater body, and the largest lake in Central America. Eventually back, and sat for a nourishing bowl of veggie soup and an orange juice, feeling good, and properly worked out. Checked mails to see if Ally had booked a flight yet, but she hadn't. Got cleaned up and changed, fired up the mozzie coil, then to a bar, but it was empty, so back to my local for a few cerveza grandes, a feed and ended up with the Austrian dude again, who's name was Michael. A criollo style desayuno, which is sort of traditional, plus my usual English breakfast tea. Avocado is widely served with most meals in the form of guacamole, so expensive in Europe, but get a dollop with just about every dish in Latin America. Pass a spell reading, then suddenly fancy some beach time. Walking to the bus stop, I was yet again bewildered by conversation with a local guy, just couldn't get what he was saying. Fuck knows whats with the Spanish here. Hitched a lift with a pick up, and jumped down to look around a finca for a while, a ranch cum farm that mostly raises or grows organic produce. Trekked to Venecia, wandering round, taking in the views, and small talk with the local women: must be laundry day, most were washing clothes in the dirty looking laguna waters. A good sweaty hike one way, then return, stopping for a juice, before getting a burn off on the beach along with a cooling swim. A walk in the nearby woods, for some great vistas of the volcano, and see lots of colourful birds, a monkey, and a massive trail of army ants: leafcutter ants also now a common sight. Waiting for the bus, I got chatting to a Yank, a relief from talking Spanish. An age before the vehicle arrives, and returns me to Moyogalpa, feeling satiated and at peace after my day in nature. Bit of a quiet night, not many people are about. Apparently there is a fiesta at a beach, but just couldn't be bothered to go; as I've said before, I must be getting old.

A rest day methinks, some reading and a gentle walk along the beach. I want to go on the island tour tomorrow, so try to book it, but there is a lot of uncertainty, something to do with the amount of other guests; he will let me know later. At the net cafe, I found out that Ally is coming on the 14th march, to San José, the capital city of Costa Rica. That's about a month from now, perfect. The mad Welshman has broken his cheek, out of his brains on drink and drugs do doubt. An early beer, chatting to a Dutch guy called Luke. Decided to eat there also, and lots wrong, tostones, fried plantains instead of papas, plus some of the food was cold. A fat local guy who wasn't wearing a shirt was really pissed off with his meal. Matey didn't show up to let me know about the tour, so assume it's not on. Couple more with Luke and another Dutch chap, but won't be eating there again.

A good breakfast at Los Ranchitos, then go to try and book a tour with another company for tomorrow. He will let me know if he gets other people by this evening. Potter, trying to decide what to do, and make my mind up to get a closer look at Volcán Maderas, which forms the eastern lump of Ometepe. Got a bus to El Quino, and start to walk to Santo Domingo, the distances are not so great. Nice jaunt through rural settlements, the road wasn't in good shape, but the locals were friendly as ever. A bus bound for San Ramon came along, so jump up for the long slow bounce there, the route was in terrible condition, barely able to call it a thoroughfare. Arrived at San Ramon at 12.30pm, and luckily, checked the return time. Only one back, at 2.30pm, which now doesn't give me enough time to hike to the cascada. Objective achieved though, a closer look at the volcano, less active and covered by cloud forest which harbours numerous species of flora and fauna.

Start the stroll back towards home, and soon reach Mérida, a small village, spotting a hacienda, and stop for an enjoyable lunch plus juice, majestic panoramas to taunt the visual receptors with. Lots of other travellers, but made no effort to engage, just wanted to gaze at the landscape surrounding me. Continued on foot, to cut down the amount of time on the bus, which pootled by at some point, and I endured the long bumpy haul to Altagracia. Watched a basketball game, whilst waiting, then onwards, reaching Moyogalpa around 6.30pm, the sun had already set by then. Quick shower, then go to find Horatio, who told me that the tour was on mañana; sweet. Back to my place for a beer, and an Hungarian guy called Dudas sought me out, also wanting to join me for the island trip. He requested some changes, so it became complicated, we will see how things pan out on the morrow? Luke joined us, which I was grateful for, Dudas seemed a bit manic. He told me he had been bitten by a vicious street dog! I'd noticed that some of them acted rather aggressively.

The gallo pinto, which means spotted rooster, but is actually beans with rice, was shit again. Went to where Dudas was staying, but Horatio hadn't arrived yet, so got an extra tea in. When he came, he told us that others had let him down, so only us two now; he said he could take us for $25 each. We were fine with that, eager to see the places, and Dudas seemed to have relaxed on the agenda, just happy to go with the flow. He turned out to be a brilliant laugh, reminding me of a friend in the UK called Jake. We visited many of the island's petroglyphs, animals and symbols carved onto rocks, and statues sculpted out of boulders, a fascinating insight into the pre Columbian inhabitants of the region, obviously quite advanced. Dudas reckoned that the petroglyphs were graffiti done by bored kids, doodling in between tending to the fields. A guided tour around a working finca, then lunch in Santo Domingo, and a dip in the lake to cool off. A longer hike through Reserva Charco Verde, where we bagged a troop of howler monkeys, chorusing their loud tumultuous cries. On the way home, we stopped at a church where there was a colony of small bats living in the rafters, such an important link in any ecosystem. A last stop at Punta Jesús Maria, for a beer watching the setting sun sink below the horizon. I spent the rest of the evening with Dudas as he was excellent company and very funny with it. Two Aussie guys, Henry and Chris, joined us for a while. They were sailing to The Galapagos islands, then onwards across the Pacific, back to Australia; sounded like a wonderful adventure. Darwin's old haunt was fully on my radar at some point.

Chris collared me the next morning over the breaking of our fast, and picked my brains about Africa, making notes, me running away with enthusiasm, talking about the wonderful trip. He had been to 63 countries, a few more than me, though I'd achieved the half century point by then. Someone who left a review on my first book, Wanderlust, said my travels seemed to be more about a country count! It is purely just a bit of fun, a talking point sometimes, a bit of gentle competition. If it was solely about clocking up visited nations, I would obviously move a lot faster, and just collect stamps in my passport. I'm genuinely interested in our world, the cultures, the natural beauty, and more so now art and architecture, etc etc; but there is no harm in silly little games, like keeping a mental note of how many countries you have been to. Well, I don't think so anyway?

Chores day, so laundry in, shave, floss and other important hygiene upkeep. Talking from a 2020 perspective now, I have seen a lot of reports recently in mainstream media about the link between ejaculation and prostate cancer. A difficult subject because people are grossed out by it. But it's quite important to address the risk, especially if you are a single guy. Certain people who I'd met on the road, had told me about it back in the early noughties, maybe preliminary research was already underway? But it seemed quite obvious to me that getting rid of your dirty water was important, even from a comfort point of view, your balls tend to ache more if you don't eject your seed. As I'd sort of made a decision not to support prostitution anymore, it was another task to perform, when you had a private room, tricky in a shared dormitary. And I wasn't seeming to be very good at pulling as I got older, most of the female travellers were much younger than me for one thing. Sorry to bring it up, excuse the pun, but there does appear to be an increased risk of prostate cancer associated with decreased incidents of sex or cracking one off.

A spell in the net cafe, seeing the Aussies again, who were leaving imminently, so goodbyes to them. Scanned the news, the world is still turning, things are settling down on the international stage; the single worry was North Korea announcing possession of nukes! I walked back to Jesús Maria to kill a couple of hours, a pleasant stroll and dip in the lake. Saw a vine snake, cool, love snakes, but don't tend to see many, and also numerous lizards. Caught the bus back, and collected my washed and dried clothes, started the process of repacking ready for moving on. A wander round looking for company, but not an abundance of tourists, and wanted to relax instead of trying to understand local Spanish. Back home for a beer and cena, a German couple who didn't want to speak to me, so all by myself with my thoughts. Suddenly, a young lady arrived, got a drink and asked if she could join me? She was Krista from Colorado, a bit overwhelmed by solo travelling, on her way to meet friends in Costa Rica. We spent the entire few hours in companionable conversation, over a few drinks, a thoroughly affable and gratifying evening.

The ferry to San Carlos was at 6pm, so I had all day to kill, and had to check out by noon, or pay another night. Two magpies were fighting in a tree, and they both plummeted to the ground, clawing and pecking each other; handbags at dawn! Chatted to a couple of Australian girls during breakfast, then passed time reading and pruning. Checked out, the girls were still about, and one had told me it was her birthday, so I gave her my travel alarm clock as a gift. Idle away an hour online, looking through the World Wildlife Fund website, some shocking statistics, and the human population of Earth has topped 6.5 billion! Bus to Altagracia, and walk along to the dock, hot and sweaty, plus lots of bugs, which is good, but can be irritating. Still only 3pm, so sit with a beer and continue with my book, working my way through Michael Crichton novels now. Got something to eat, then went to purchase my right of passage, the day was drawing to a close. Could see the boat lights heading in our direction, and it parked up about 6.30, the cargo began to be loaded and us passengers were ushered onboard. We sailed at 7.30, only an hour and a half late, not too bad in these countries. Still tons of insects when I went up to the top deck, to view the night sky, even seeing a couple of shooting stars. Found a seat, and got a few fitful, fairly uncomfortable hours slumber, stopping twice during the voyage, and landed in San Carlos about 6ish the following morning, just getting light again.

It was easy to find the second dock for transportation to El Castillo, but not a craft until 8am. Checked out migration, and onwards travel to Costa Rica, will be coming back this way in a day or two. A bite to eat with a Dutch couple, who I'd met in Tegucigalpa, and then it was time to sail. I sat with a husband and wife from Vancouver, who I thought might be Mum and Dad's friends, but they weren't; that would have been off the scale of incredible coincidence. The river ride was unbelievably amazing, an absolute abundance of bird life especially, but other wildlife also. Blue and white herons, storks, cormorants, egrets, teals, coots and ducks, gulls and terns. Eagles, kingfishers, sandpipers, pelicans and spoonbills, all in copious numbers. Lots of colourful birds that no one knew the names of, wading birds of unknown species, and obviously never got round to looking them up. Thousands of swallows feeding on the wing, insects in their billions, literally tons of them. River turtles and caymans, fish jumping from the water to catch bugs that are near the surface. A stretch of the river with trees along the banks, completely enveloped in massive spider webs, the whole ecosystem teeming with life; how the whole planet would have been pre Homo sapien. Felt like I'd travelled back in time a million years. The journey alone has made that excursion worthwhile, even if it's an utterly shit destination. It wasn't. We had stopped at a few small villages during the mind-blowing voyage, to drop off and pick up passengers. Finally we were told that we had arrived in El Castillo, where the passage ended, a sweet and tranquil settlement with guest houses right on the waterfront, and rapids a little way down the course of the San Juan. Got lunch, and a wander, more agriculture there, but all looked organic to me. Chickens pecked about, and fish was a mainstay of dietary protein. A siesta to imbed the images in my mind's eye, very serene dreams, and an immense feel good factor on awakening. I met Gary, an American, who was okay, but my bullshit sensors were alerted after a while, his tales started to become a bit outlandish. A Danish couple who didn't speak great Spanish invited me to join them for a trip into the reserve tomorrow, so we went to book it. I spent the evening with Gary, drinking a few beers and eating a camarones or shrimp meal, his stories never let up, he'd literally been everywhere and done everything. The hardened jungle explorer, Gary, was sick in the night. Along the road for breaky, and got going below the small cataracts, hugging the Costa Rica border now, thick, lush tropical forest on both sides, and caymans spotted, lazing on the muddy river beaches. We got some more tea thankfully in one of the few huts at the entrance to Refugio Bartola, part of the Reserva Biológica Indio Maiz. We were issued wellies, it was going to be muddy apparently, and so it was. Our guide arrived, and we set off along a trail into the dense woodland, of an amazing variety of tree species, bromeliads, ferns, mosses, plentiful vines, other interesting flora including orchids. Another incredible day of wildlife viewing, tiny red tree frogs, parrots, spider monkeys, more small caymans, army ants, butterflies and dragonflies. Repellant was essential, lots of biting insects also present, and even got bitten wearing it. Jaguar spoor, in the form of poo and paw prints, quite fresh; oh my God, a chance at a sighting of that so elusive of all the big cats. It wasn't to be, unfortunately, but it's still thrilling to be in their habitat, maybe one was watching us, hidden in a tree? A first for me was basilisks, or Jesus lizards, that literally run across water when you spook them, or to escape predators. Saw many on that little jolly into the jungle. We were served a big lunch included in the price of the tour, then taken back to below the rapids, and a short stroll back to the digs. Didn't feel like eating again later, so just a couple coldies, listening to more of Gary's tall tales, then early to sleep.

There was a 6am boat back to San Carlos, I had to wake up the family that ran the guest house to get out. Slower going upstream, about five hours for the return journey, with some stops. The amount of insects was mind boggling, I had never seen anything quite like it, even in Kruger, the numbers were more likely into the trillions, making an excellent base of the food chain, and the reason why all other life is in such abundance. Back in SC, got my Nicaragua exit stamp, another unexpected $4.

COSTA RICA AND PANAMÁ.

The next vessel was scheduled to leave at midday, so I bought a ticket and had something to eat. Another nice boat ride on the Rio Frio, meaning cold, to Los Chiles in Costa Rica. Got chatting to a couple of guys, and we sighted more caymans, turtles and kingfishers. Immigration was straightforward, just stamps; then found the bus, of a better standard now, instead of chicken buses, to Ciudad Quesada. Nothing special about the landscape, mostly agriculture, so caught up on a bit of sleep. A police check, got a feeling that was going to be commonplace. Taxi to hotel del Norte, all fine, it was raining a lot on and off. Go for food and just the one beer, then an evening with the tele, which helped me to sleep again.

Had managed to avoid drawing any more cash in Nicaragua, I was down to just a few dollars, so the main job was getting money. No problem here, plenty of ATMs, a more western society, catering for the American tourist. 100,000 colones, was about £110, always a relief when you are fuelled up with funds, so treated myself to a decent breaky, English black tea readily available it seemed. Checked out and walked to the station, queueing to ride the bus to La Fortuna, about an hour and a half. A lot of folk look American or European or caucasian I suppose, even in the way they dress, maybe they are migrants from The States over the decades? A lot more people speak American English for sure, which didn't bode well for keeping up the Spanish practise, though I endeavoured to have conversations in that language each day, and it was easier to comprehend there. Hostel Dorothy was nice, and opted for a slightly more expensive single room, with en suite. The town was very touristy, lots of adventure activities, reminded me of Queenstown in New Zealand. But I'm scouting for now, for when Ally arrives in less than a month's time. Horrible mosquitoes, tiny little fuckers, that you can barely see, and leave an extremely itchy welt. Went upmarket for dinner, and got stung by a 22 percent tax, gonna have to be careful about that in future. Fancied some diving, so picked a place to head to, and to recce for when Ally comes. Three and a half hours on bad roads to Tilaran, the bus traversing around the shoreline of Lake Arenal, with pretty views, and more perfect cone shaped volcanoes. A tout sold me a ticket for onwards travel to Cañas, he turned out to be kosher, and we were moving again. Got dropped at the junction, and straight onto another for Liberia, chatting to a Canadian who was quite hard work. We walked together to hotel Liberia, okay rooms and cheap enough. Bit of net time, then a read of my new science mag someone had given me. Later, I went to eat, and met a Polish guy called Andre? He was with some local Costa Ricans, and he suggested I join them, to go and dine at a good place they knew of. We got on it after our food, and ended up at the casino, drinking rum until 3am the following morning, played some chess, and had to bat off the seductions of the working girls, trying to stick to my new rule, quite difficult after a few, and they were very attractive ladies.

Was supposed to meet up with Andre and co, but my sober sensible head told me to keep advancing late forenoon. Got a meal and some tea, then taxied to the terminal, and rode the transport to Playa del Coco. Lovely place, a lad on the bus took me to a decent, cheapish guest house, then I went to enquire about some diving. The shop was Summer-Salt, a nice play on words I thought; Rosemary seemed very profesional, and I met Rick from London doing his advanced who assured me it was the outfit to book with. Some blessed beach time, topping up the tan, and the sea was pleasantly warm. Fantastic views around the bay, lots of boats, and worryingly, jet skies, a menace to marine life in my opinion. Went for a few early ones with Rick, good convo, then back for a shower. Saw

Rick again later, was planning a quiet night, but they looked to be having fun so I joined them. At some point, reason took hold, something I liked about getting older, and I went to the toilet, sneaking out afterwards, returning to the digs for some kip.

Just shy of a hangover, so drink a litre of water, then get some recuperating tea. A paltry breakfast next door, and to the dive shop, where they were experiencing problems with their boat. Arrangements were made whilst we got some kit sorted, and shortly on our way to Punta Argentina, for a 20 metre depth dive with a small group for nearly an hour. Logged panamic green moray eel and a free swimming jewel moray, a lot of firsts for me again. Cornetfish, hawkfish, a shoal of grunts; seahorses, one of my favourites, such an intriguing life cycle. King angelfish, southern stingrays, that had fish pecking at them, maybe to remove parasites? Tortuga, our second dive site, which means turtle in Spanish, was close to 20 metres also, but, alas, no reptiles. But some other amazing sightings; octopuses, a bloody frogfish, very difficult to see, such incredible camouflage. More morays, scorpionfish, lobsters and stingrays. An absorbing wreak with a myriad of reef fish living inside the wheelhouse. All in all, very satisfied and added immensely to my wildlife species numbers viewed in their natural habitats.

Back to land, and walking along the beach, there was a dead stingray washed up, that gulls were in the process of devouring. Quick couple of beers with Rick, liked a drink that one, man after my own heart. Later, got my log book stamped up, and a bit of looking through identifying encyclopedias, and another swifty with Rick, he was extremely good company, very knowledgeable and easy to talk to. A shower, and change of clothes, then met four Americans staying at the hostel from Pennsylvania and Ohio, so sat chatting and supping with them. Bar Loco for a feed, and Rick was there, so several more over several hours, tunes quite loud, but mellifluous; exchanged email, and tottered home after midnight.

Bit of a lie in, then food, and go say goodbyes to the dive crowd, a good bunch of people, common within the diving fraternity.

Long wait for a bus, then make the mistake of getting down at Sardinal, thinking I could go the back road, but no transport that way! Another long wait, getting a bite to eat, then to Filadelfia, Belén, and finally to Huacas. Fuck me, that seemed to be more difficult than it should have been. A couple were going to Tamarindo, but not till later, so I hitched a lift with a pick up truck to end the calamity of that day's travel; such a short distance had taken so long. Nice enough place, very touristy, mostly loud holidaying Yanks, and the beachfront was all hotels and restaurants, don't think I will bring Ally here. Go for beer and eats, look along the playa, but the whole place has a false feel to it.

The mosquitoes in the night denied me a great deal of sleep, so I was tired and didn't feel like moving. For a touristy place, I still had trouble finding a book exchange, working internet and a cheap phone card system! Got a gringo breakfast at an American diner, and decided on a good walk along the beach to fill my day. It was a Saturday, so heaps of people, and can only go so far as a fast flowing river runs into the sea, and no bridge to cross over it. Walk back and as far as I can the other way, about three quarters of an hour. Swim, sunbathe and read a bit; it became windy, and lots of human traffic, so not really relaxing. The hostel was now full, as it's the weekend, but managed to sit with a couple of musicians from Argentina, speaking a combination of English and Spanish, or what is sometimes called Spanglish. Go to eat and just a couple, then back and have to wait for the noisy neighbours to go out, before spraying up the room, killing dozens of mossies, ventilating a bit, then a better sleep.

Ablutions and away early, the shop was still closed, so no bananas. Managed to catch the first departure for Santa Cruz, giving myself a chance of making it to San José. Pithered and dithered all the way there, stopping and starting, people constantly getting off or embarking: so a few painful hours to arrive! Looking around the station for my next, but couldn't find it, so asked others and turned out to be from another terminal. Fucking pain, every town is different, so never know what to do. It wasn't far, so I walked it, and just missed one leaving and, being a Sunday, the next was a while's wait! Frustrating as fuck. I'm already thinking that when Ally is here, we will hire a car, can't show her around like this, she's only got two weeks. Got some pasties to eat, and eventually get going again, but by the time we pulled into Nicoya, I'd had enough. Checked into hotel Chorotega situated by a nice parque, good and cheap, with en suite. Couldn't get my haircut, all the shops were shut including the cyber cafes. Found a restaurant with a public computer, but failed to log on to my hotmail! It was hot, and I was getting pissed off with everything not going right, I needed to take five. I sat with a few beers and a meal on an upstairs terrace, watching the never ending stream of traffic, the air smelt, and again, I puzzled as to where people are going, endlessly, perpetually, incessantly, nonstop: permanently?

Great sleep, no mossies, no noise, caught up fully at long last. To the bus station, and grab a small bunch of little, stubby sweet bananas, always think about Pablo in Bolivia when I buy them. The transport to San José was rammed, so had to stand, with armpits in your face, making sure someone is not trying to pick your pockets. A girl beckoned me to sit next to her when somebody got down, and no one challenged, so I took it, entering into conversation with her. About four hours, with a short fag break, dry and parched landscape, all agricultural, then some hilly country with vegetation, but looks like deforestation was underway. People still threw trash out of the windows, in this country that promotes ecotourism! It was not any more so than other Central American nations as far as I could see. Just a gimmick, to overcharge gullible Americans more money to visit small National parks? Hopefully the south would be better? A three quarter of a kilometre long suspension bridge over the river Tempisque was impressive, and a symbol to global friendship. Taxi to El Descanso hotel, good and central, and out for lunch. Haircut, internet, and an exploration of my new location, a reasonably pleasant city on the whole. Hygiene chores, and a good read up of the LP, sussing out a plan of sorts. Beers and food; on the way home, there were a lot of people gathered around a big screen in a square, watching a football game between Costa Rica and El Salvador, which CR won 2-1.

My present local was Manolo's, good food at an acceptable cost, and they could knock me up a lovely cuppa. To terminal Caribe, finding the big bus to Guapiles, chicken buses no longer the norm, they were all modern style coaches, though still polluting diesel powered. The road went through the National park, so the driver paid the toll, included in the ticket price no doubt. I jumped down at Quebrada González ranger station, where I collected some leaflets of the trails. Climbing into beautiful cloud forest habitat, lush wet tropical vegetation abounded, dripping sounds constant from the canopy, the stuff of life, germinating the giddying array of flora, and you just know that all manner of fauna is proliferating productively, profusely to multiply in the never ending cycle of existence; biology and vitality and vigour breathed through the burgeoning growth of vines, bromeliads, ferns, mosses and massive trees. Colonies of leaf cutter ants worked the forest, forever recycling the matter; many birds were heard and a few were seen, lizards darting undercover as they detected your presence.

At a bridge where two rivers merge, the colour of the Rio Sucio was yellow from sulphur deposits upstream, the minerals laid down by volcanic activity, the other course was clear and both were fast flowing. I met a couple from Wisconsin, and joined them for a short loop walk. Afterwards, I started another track, but it was very muddy, and didn't really have the right footwear, so turned back. Got good views of a stretch of the yellow river, and could see a road bridge in the far distance. Feeling refreshed, once again realising that nature is a fantastic uplifting tonic, stimulating brain chemistry and electricity, I started the return journey to San José. I checked out a few hostels in the city, trying to find one with twin private rooms, to keep the cost down, knowing Ally wouldn't want to stay in shared dormitories. Collected my peachy clean laundry, a shower, and back to Manolo's for a feed and a couple of beers.

After eating and sipping tea, I now seemed to be considered a valuable regular customer at Manolo's, I went to find the conveyance to Volcán Poás: it was $5 for a return, a bit of a bonus. Through Alajuela, then back into the countryside, climbing up switchback roads, to the parking lot quite near the summit. So a short walk to the caldera, but we entered the cloud, so only fleeting glimpses of the crater lakes. A nice hike around the cloud forest nature trail, seeing some hummingbirds, and tried to get photos, but they didn't come out very well. Squirrels and other birds feeding and bathing in the puddles, looking out for frogs and snakes that are common, but no luck, some loud talking Yanks put pay to that. Browsed the informative visitor centre, always picking up snippets of knowledge in those halls of fact about the local area. Back in San José, I'm trying to conserve funds as it's going to be more expensive when Ally is here, so a bit of tv, reading then a cheap feed of sopa and a pollo con arroz, frijoles y plantains main, plus the obligatory couple of coldies of course. Costa Rica were playing Panama, nil nil until the dying minutes of the game, then CR scored to eruptions of cheers.

There was a beggar guy pretending to play a flute, his feet were in a terrible state. Two blokes gave him some bread, but he just threw it away, ungrateful blighter. After eating at my local, last time for now, I checked out and a quite long walk to the terminal for transport south, and embarked on the journey to San Isidro de El General. The lady conductor made me move from my window seat for some reason, which was a bit irksome; I like to scan the landscape on bus rides. There was an accident on the highway, which held things up, but didn't look like fatalities luckily. The countryside was hilly, and could be beautiful, but was totally put over to agriculture, only small pockets of protected land visible. I was finding out that there was lots of legal and illegal logging going on anyway, so the great eco friendly Costa Rica was just the same as every other country in the world, destroying its biodiversity slowly but surely.

San Isidro was a nice town, and the Astoria hotel was basic but cheap and clean. Bit of lunch and pineapple juice, internet and other chores. Checked out the station for onwards, all easy peasy. About 6pm, I went for dinner and three beers, the traffic the same as always, just a continuous stream of cars, trucks and buses. Reckon the human race will evolve to have no legs, most don't seem capable of walking anymore. I'm not seeing the ecological superiority that I'd been led to believe Costa Rica was? Sure, there are some amazing parks, teeming with wildlife, but the general perception that it is a first rate environmental nation, peerless in its approach to protecting nature, wasn't altogether evident to me. With all the problems in this world, it appeared that Costa Ricans had become prosperous on the back of ecotourism, and with their new found wealth, become abusive of the nature that they were earning a living from; there's got to be a price to pay for those excesses in the future? There was a full moon that eventually showed its face and brilliance after hiding behind clouds most of the evening.

I caught a bus to Dominical after eating, on the Pacific west coast. Spent a couple of hours checking out all the cabañas, finding a perfect place to stay for $35 a twin. This is where I'm going to bring Ally first off, a nice peaceful place with a lovely beach, and not too crowded. Plenty of bars and cafes, and much to do in the local vicinity. Trying to cut down on the fags yet again, so buying single sticks, and savouring each one, but keeping the number a day under ten. Good walk up and down the beach, a bit of swimming and sunbathing, keeping the body colour a decent tone. The locals are friendly, and a smattering of other foreign tourists, got chatting to a Canadian girl. Bit more catching up with mail and news, then a quiet evening with a feed and a few, contemplating life generally, there was no one else to talk to.

Currency resupplied, breaky, check out, and catch a bus to Uvita. The lad sitting next to me got down but forgot his bag, so I dropped it out of the window for him. Everywhere was expensive, double the price in the guide book! Tourist information tried to find me somewhere cheaper, but most places were full. Leave my bag there, and go ask around, and the best I can do is hire a tent for the night, clean, quite pleasant, the weather was good and it was cheap. Into the Marino Ballena National park, ballena means whale in Spanish, and the spit of land that protrudes out to sea, looks incredibly like a whale's tail. There are also migrating humpback whales that use the ocean there for breeding purposes, the warm tropical waters are ideal, before they head north for their summer feeding grounds. Walked up and down the remote beach, and out onto the tail, for terrific views of the inland jungle and the vast Pacific. A huge formation of pelicans plus blue herons, frigatebirds and ibises. Back through the forest, leafcutter ants and lizards galore, birdsong and monkey calls I think. The tide had come in, so had to wade across the river to get back, brown scum floating on the surface which I suspected was human waste. Good clean up, and change of clothes, then for the evening meal, and a few, hardly anyone else about, a real sleepy place, even on a Saturday night in high season.

Didn't sleep too bad in the tent, a bit hot, but no bugs disturbing me. Bit more checking out of places to stay, getting business cards with phone numbers, to make reservations, don't want disappointments when Ally is here. The hotel Tucán was smashing, stunning gardens and saw my first wild toucan birds, such ravishing looking creatures. Chat with Mark from Portsmouth, who was working there, over breakfast and tea. Even managed to exchange a reading book. I bought a phone card, the first booth didn't work, so I had to hunt down another. Tried to call Ally, but no answer, so rang Mum and Dad, really hot as not in the shade. The credit ran out, so I went to buy one more, and later phoned Ally again, getting to talk that time, she was really looking forward to coming, excitement in her voice. Rest of the day on the beach, with plenty of cooling swims, the tide eventually forced me back, but stayed for the sunset, which was glorious. A few surfer dudes rode the waves, very impressed with their skills on the boards. A beautiful place, so many sea birds, the frigatebirds in great numbers, with a striking red throat sac that the male inflates to attract a female. Scientists have studied their flight, so aerobatic, that they try to design an aircraft wing similar, but no great success as yet. Spent part of the evening with Georgia, the Canadian girl, but it's not a party place, so fairly early to bed. In the darkness near the tent, I saw thousands of tiny lights, flickering on and off, which were fireflies: that was spectacular, and I sat watching them for an hour or more, mesmerised.

Another guy had pitched a tent nearby to me, so chatted with him, then went to a soda to eat. The bird feeders in the grounds were very busy with all manner of avians, of all sizes and colours. Jays, thrushes, tanagers, hummingbirds and so many more that I didn't identify, just enjoying the breathtaking display, remarkable amount of species in this biodiversity hotspot of the world; just hope that it gets better protection, it really deserves to be safeguarded vigorously. Packed up, and to the road, waiting in the shade of a tree for the bus, with a few others. It came about 11am, and the road was good, the distance short, so soon into Ciudad Cortés, then Palmar Norte ten minutes later. A nice room at Lok Sek cabinas, only three mil, then a wander round the town, seeing some pre Columbian sculptures and stone orbs, that haven't been fully worked out yet. Spell in the net cafe, and a walk to the river bridge over the Térraba, sighting many kingfishers in the trees along the banks. Finish Sphere, another Crichton novel, science fiction cum thriller, more food for thought on the human psyche, then began Horse Whisperer by Nicholas Evans. An okay chinky feed, and a couple at a quiet bar, I'm definitely liking the south of Costa Rica more, it's certainly more natural.

Where I ate was where the bus departed from, but not until 9.15am. More tourists on that one, a popular thing to do in Costa Rica, visiting and hiking a part of the peninsula that is Corcovado National park. The journey took us through the Golfo Dulce forest reserve, the roads not great, but heaps of jungle vegetation; giant ceiba trees, and all other types as mentioned before, luxuriant, dense and verdant. Puerto Jiménez was a small town, just catering for people wanting to trek the NP. Got a simple cabin, meeting a Dutch couple who have just returned, very enthusiastic about the excursion, which heightened my own zeal. Go to drink a juice with them, jotting down all the info they threw at me. Got registered, and made reservations for an overnight stay at a campsite. Trouble procuring a hired tent, but hunt one down eventually. Went to feed the caymans, seeing a fair few, waiting for the chicken scraps we bunged in the water for them. Also, many egrets, herons and lizards; parrots and toucans also spied. Spent the evening with a biologist, studying the region, an interesting and educational couple of hours. Restlessness brought on by excited anticipation made sleep difficult, but drifted off finally, and got a few hours.

Up at 4.30am, ablutions, stashed a bag, and to the stand for transport back to La Palma. I'd bought snacks and fruit to eat, plus plenty of water, all in a pack with the tent strapped beneath. I was the only one at the colectivo, a pick up truck, and it was 12 mil to the start of the trail, so I waited, and luckily, four Dutch guys turned up, so we shared the cost. Many rivers to cross, a wild and bumpy ride, though the scenery was sublime. An initial 2.5 kilometre easy walk to Los Patos where you check in, recording all your details in a log. I let the others get a good head start, as I wanted to stroll along on my own, quietly, giving myself a better chance to see the animals. A full day's hike through the rainforest, then dry tropical woodland, marvelling at the diversity of plant life. Bagged lots of stuff, vine snakes, parrot snakes, so many different lizard species; new world primates including white faced capuchins, squirrel and howler monkeys. Macaws and toucans, a family of large pheasants, could hear woodpeckers more or less constantly. Dart frogs, agoutis, scanning the higher boughs for sloths, but didn't see any.

Then, I could hear some noises further up the track, so I started to edge forward, in a semi crouch, keeping completely silent, and I saw my first coatis, a troop of about twenty odd, browsing the undergrowth. I sat down observing for a long while, they seemed to be oblivious of my presence, and still moving slowly towards me, giving me a good look at them. I was spotted suddenly, and the cries of danger rang out, sending the whole troop to the treetops. I'd been busted, so I got up and continued on my way, to leave them in peace, fully satisfied with my ten to fifteen minutes witnessing their foraging. I rocked up at Sirena ranger station about four in the afternoon, pitched the tent and sat chatting to the Dutch guys, and a couple from Slovenia, eating crisps, crackers and picking the ticks out of my skin. There was no lyme disease in that area luckily, an infection caused by bacteria spread by ticks, but you had to be careful prising out the head, so it didn't break off, possibly resulting in infection. A well needed shower, and tried to view the night sky, but too many bugs were active, so retired to the tent, which was hot inside, but cooled as the evening wore on, and got a surprisingly better sleep than expected.

Up at the crack of dawn, breaking camp, and embarked on the second day of tough walking, muscles in my legs easing out as I got going. Changed into sandals to wade across the Rio Claro, and got chatting to an Aussie lady, who told me a tapir had been glimpsed at the water's edge. I hung around for a bit, in hope of its return, but it was probably spooked by the human nearness. Hiked for hours, including a long stretch down a beach, which was gruelling because of the heat and soft sand. Eventually back onto a forest trail, but the trudge on the beach has taken its toll, my legs and feet suffering, and sweating buckets. Some climbs around coastal headlands made the going even more punishing, but saw some more wildlife; monkeys, macaws, and woodpeckers. De-ticking at rest stops, guzzling water and eating energy bars. There was some fresh water available at one point, so I gorged on it, filling the bottles also. Beautiful clear blue ocean views a pleasurable companion, to take my mind off the arduous toil. After an age, the signs in kms, but they seemed like miles, I reached La Leona camp, the Dutch boys looked fucked as well. Got a lovely refreshing mango juice at the eco lodge, then a final three kilometres to Carate, along a firmer beach, on the flat, so quite an easy last push.

Back in relative civilisation, and places to sit and eat a meal, waiting for a taxi to return us to town. A long slow drive back to Puerto Jiménez, seeing a mammal that resembled a badger, and some more caymans. Returned the tent, getting my deposit back, and checked into the cabin again, sorting my stuff out, and having a blissful cold shower, luckily no actual blistering on my feet, just soreness. My body was screaming out for a cold beer, so I succumbed gratefully, and had a fantastic meal also, then a few with some English lads who were going on the trek tomorrow. Two

Martins, a Rob and an Eddie, plus the Australian women and her friend talking about climbing Cerro Chirripó, Costa Rica's highest peak, something I was considering. Read a while back at the digs, then slept like the dead.

Up at 8am, feeling refreshed, legs aching not surprisingly. Local breakfast and many teas, there was a bus at 11am, so no particular hurry. I wanted to see a bit of the Caribbean side, just to check out if there was anywhere else I could show Ally, but there's not a direct route, a mountain range runs through the middle of the country, so I would have to return to San José. The desired transport didn't happen for whatever reason, and next wasn't until 1pm! Expensive internet session, two mil an hour, and the connection was painfully slow. Met two guys from Chicago on the bus, they got down at Palmar Norte, and I continued to San Isidro, taking hours with all the stopping and starting, pithering and shilly-shallying. Arrived after sunset, and back to the Astoria, meeting another Yank with a load of problems that he wanted to share. Dump stuff in the room, and sneak back out, desperate to avoid matey, going to my old local for a good feed and three beers.

An easy day's travel, just three hours to San José; shared a taxi to Tranquillo hostel with a chap from Oregon. Most important job was to put laundry in, so that done, go for a wander. There was a good crowd staying at the backpackers, Joe who I'd met earlier was an environmentalist, so had common ground with him. An English girl called Lydia; Ryan and Julia who I'd met at Playa del Coco. Get my clean clothes back, read a bit, try to watch the news on the tv, but only American CNN, not really very informative about global affairs. Went to eat and a couple, then back with some take outs, for a pleasant evening on the outside balcony, even a little un doing the rounds, so got some quite intense conversation, and a bit of laughing and joking to round the night off with.

The free breakfast included with the cost of the bed was of an American nature, naturally; pancakes and syrup. There was milk and I had tea bags, so I could drink my fill of my favourite morning beverage. Many others, hostels are or were very sociable places, and pre the smartphone, people actually conversed with each other. So I was engaged in chat with an American lady called Theresa and an Austrian bloke. I'd been on a top bunk the previous night, but I prefered the bottom ones, but they had all been occupied. Someone left, and I exchanged beds, after clean sheets were installed. San José is an agreeable enough city, so I strolled around looking at the plazas, with some fine colonial architecture, churches and cathedrals. Not the best in Central America, but sufficiently charming to warrant a few hours. Costa Rica, like Australia, was to me more about nature and wildlife. I reckoned the zoo would be good there, but was left disappointed. Pitiful really, not terrible, but not at all good either, supposed to be promoting awareness of conservation, but it was a pretty lame attempt at portraying the ideology of preservation.

Later, back at the hostel, I met a Swiss guy called Angelo, who invited me to join him for a drink in a bar he knew. Pretty sure it was a gay joint, the barman was definately suss, and I didn't feel particularly comfortable, so made my excuses and returned to the backpackers. Chatted to Catherine just arrived from the UK, a journalist, so she brought me up to speed on current affairs. A toke with Angelo, and a Danish bird nerd, then Joe came back after a day out, and also Ryan, Julia and Lydia joined us, so ended up having a decent night of chat, anecdote, fun and mirth. Suddenly, a firework display began on the roof of a nearby building, which went on for quite some time, crescendoing in an intense finale, that left us spellbound for a while. I was flagging, so retired, Lydia followed me into the dorm, and turned the lights on, talking loudly, searching through bags for skins, whilst others were trying to sleep! One of the downsides of hosteling.

Ryan had left me a little pressie, bless him. Teas and sickly breaky, check out, and to terminal Caribe to rendevouz with the 9am bus to Cariari, traversing through the splendid National park Braulio Carrillo again. I bought the bus/ boat ticket to Tortuguero, $10, departing about 11.30am; chatting to a couple from Wantage whilst waiting, and a guy working on a turtle program, which I might come back to volunteer on when Ally has returned home.

Before entering the NP, we had to get down and disinfect our shoes, and the bus drove through a dip. Nice jungle setting on the boat ride, but didn't clock many birds and only saw one croc. There were touts for accommodation, and I specified I needed cheap, and ended up with a decent room near the beach, in a guest house run by Miguel. Got a feed, and on the way back, I met Gregory, who was the local dealer, and could get me some charlie, which I fancied for a change, when in Rome and all that. He also said he could take me on a canoe trip tomorrow through the mangrove forests. I went for a smoke with him on the beach, he had a dark side to him, and seemed to take offence when I spoke. On the way back, pretty wrecked, it was good gear no doubt, he shinnied up a coconut tree, plucked one, and back on the ground, he smashed it open for me. I became very paranoid, it looked like, in the dim lighting, that he was dashing someone's brains out! I got back to the room pronto, and locked the door securely behind me.

Gregory no show, so wait a bit, eating nearby so I could keep a lookout for him. Nah, he's not coming. Have to ration book reading, as no exchange place that I've seen, so read up about Panamá in the LP instead. A walk down the beach, and a swim, then lie on the sand trying to discreetly tan my white bits. The headland was a postcard perfect palm tree lined stretch of coastline, no one else about, the Robinson Crusoe feeling came over me. Oh shit, just read that it's not advisable to enter the sea here, there are sharks present in the vicinity. I hadn't gone very far out as the surf was quite big, the waves powerful, and fully conscious of things like rip tides that can catch you out. Wander back for a siesta, it was one of those extremely chilled out places, most people were toking, and very laid back to the point of being horizontal.

Later, I went to a local bar for a couple and saw Marcus who I met in El Salvador with a rasta man from Chile. Greg came by and spotted me, he wanted to get me five grams, saying that's the minimum; it was cheap so I said yes. He told me that his mum had to go to hospital, but can we do the canoe trip tomorrow? Okay, I was keen to see some of the local nature. We went to the basketball court and smoked a spliff, then got some more beer, and sat in the playground, obviously I was paying for all this. There was some confusion about the coke thing, and I said not to worry about it, getting put off by all the clandestine goings on, and starting to think it wasn't such a great idea. He went off anyway, so I waited a while, then went to the beach for my last beer, enjoying the clear night sky in the complete darkness. A madman, or very spaced out individual was frolicking in the surf, he looked like he was naked, but he was oblivious to anyone else or anything for that matter; hell of a trip he was on.

Gregory arrived a bit early, so we had some breakfast next door. The proprietor of the cafe whispered to me when I was paying that I shouldn't trust Greg, he was a known local criminal. Well, I wanted to go anyway, I would just take the bare minimum with me, and I told the guy what we were doing in case anything untoward happened. He hadn't got the nose candy, which I was actually relieved about. We spent a pleasurable three hours around the waterways, creeks and rivulets, mangrove forest abundant, and lots of wildlife. Lots of birds including a nesting tiger heron, caymans and a big iguana in a tree. Red frogs, monkeys and many lizard species which Gregory was surprisingly knowledgeable about. A short walk where I was a bit nervous; that would have been the time he would have done something if that was his intention. He did all the rowing, and his muscles were well defined, he was many years younger than me, so I would have been in trouble if he decided to kill me. But no, he seemed a different person that morning, joyful and good company.

He wanted more than we had agreed, so he could go and visit his mother in hospital, and said he would be staying over, and I thought it was worth the extra cost so he wouldn't be around that evening. I took advantage of another walk into the NP, as I'd bought an entrance ticket already. A guy had lost his glasses, and I found them on my hike, returning them to the booth on my way out. Sat on the beach for a while, two girls rode past on horseback, cantering through the surf, waving at me as they went by. There was a big iguana on the track, I thought it was dead as it didn't move on my approach. I gently prodded it with a stick, but it didn't move, so I tried to pick it up, and it suddenly came to life, running away and crashing through the undergrowth; got my heartbeat up for a few seconds. I read all the info at the ranger station, trying to educate myself about the local area of immense natural importance. Back at the digs, Greg showed up, wanting to go for a drink, I didn't even bother asking him what happened about going to the hospital, most likely all bullshit. I paid as usual, and we went to the beach for a toke, the dangerous element of his character resurfacing. He wanted even more money, he was becoming a right royal klingon. I will leave tomorrow, it's getting unrelaxing, feeling fraught every time I see him.

My resolve to skip town was still strong, another day of trying to avoid Greg in this two horse borough was unappealing at best. Tried to find Miguel to pay what I owed, but ended up leaving the cash with the cafe owner. Bought my boat/ bus right of passage back to Cariari, and waited an age, worrying that Gregory was going to find me and cause a fuss. A gay guy or women, wasn't 100 percent sure, sat with me to chat, and the vessel eventually docked about 11am. Phew, we were away. Saw three caymans, many birds and of course millions of bugs on the nice ride back. The bus driver was agitated as I was supposed to get the fare from the boat skipper, but another guy helped me sort it out. It was hot, and people seemed worked up, unfriendly, short with me, maybe because of the heat. The lady at the hotel had been rude, but she tried to make amends later, contrite about her behaviour. Catch up with mail, Ally will be here in a few days, and a plan was almost fully formed by now. Found an old copy of National Geographic to read, my book finished, and will have to wait until I'm back in San José to exchange. Subdued couple with a feed, quiet to the point of being boring.

Will head back to SJ methinks, at least I will be in a hostel with other travellers. A nice breaky, and got tea how I like it, I'm using my Spanish more again, a bit of rustiness had crept in. There wasn't a bus till 11.30am, so I amused myself by showing a bunch of kids my world map and Spanish books, basically giving a geography and English lesson to them, donating the map to their school on an impulse. Scenic couple of hours back, returning to the Tranquillo, getting the same bed as before. Angelo and Lydia were still there, some German girls and American ladies. Second hand book shop for a browse, then a spell in the net cafe. A KFC for a change, not too bad for once. A reasonably tame evening with the crowd, a few drinks and a smoke, then to the basement to finish the night off, but nothing really happening.

Still felt a bit stoned, but chilled, and in a lazy mood, not planning anything in particular. Back on the pancakes, they are included, so silly not to. Pay another two nights, and settle into a dossy sort of day, only task necessary was to visit the ATM. A preacher man was exhorting people to repent their sins, better not go there. Angelo had one on the go out on the balcony, so that determined how the rest of the day played out. Various people came and went, sitting for a chat, and we steadily drank through the afternoon and evening, until fatigue overcame me about 10pm.

Made a reservation for the twin room for tomorrow night, the reason I had chosen Tranquillo hostel. Couldn't face a high carb morning meal, so out for an American one at the News cafe. I phoned Ally just to check that all was well, and she was definitely still coming, she will arrive about 9pm tomorrow. A similar sort of day to yesterday, lots of good company, Pete and Nick from London, David from Dublin, Cathy from Essex and later Russ from Canada. We all went out for a feed at San Pedros, meeting up with some friends of Cathy's. Then a taxi back, picking up some beer from a shop en route. The older American ladies ended up being my companions for the evening, surprisingly good humoured and interesting to talk with.

MUST REMEMBER TO MEET ALLY TONIGHT AT THE AIRPORT, FLIGHT DL865, 21.30. Dorm syndrome got me up prematurely, and drank a load of tea, nibbling at the pancakes. I moved to the room late in the morning, then went to my old local Manolo's for lunch. Read and siesta, lovely having a private room again. Hung out with some others, and just made something simple to eat, sipping at a couple, needing to stay sober. A bus to the airport, nice and early, checked out the flight board, all was fine, and looked to be ontime. No bar, so a short bus ride to Alujuela, just about walking distance if need be, and got a cheeseburger and fries, then sat in a bar, until the time came to return. Half hour late in the end, then there she was, dressed in her colourful clothes with a rucksack on her back. Big hug, and a taxi back, got her settled, and introduced her to the few others still there, but tiredness demanded quite an early night.

We talked about hiring a car, but probably just for the second week Ally is here. She was keen for some beach time first off, so we could bus there, not really needing a vehicle just yet. Last pancake breakfast for a while I hope, then to the terminal and ride the transport to San Isidro, and another to Dominical, all too easy thankfully. I'd made reservations for the place I wanted us to stay, something I rarely do on my own, but want to make sure everything is a bit special for Ally. That's it then, time to kick back and relax, the holiday as opposed to a travel experience had started. An interval at the glorious seaside, Ally lathering on the sunscreen until her skin gets a bit of colour, having come from a Northern European winter. Showed her round for a bit, and got a slightly upmarket dinner. Then we had a proper good catch up on our veranda, the night time chirping of the tropics, our backstory, the balmy air and a drop or two of wine lubricated the conversation, and before we knew it, it was gone midnight.

The gardens were lush, and teeming with wildlife, iguanas, some pretty big, and tons of smaller lizards and geckos. Toucans in the treetops, Ally was amazed, many beautiful birds including iridescent hummingbirds; she was in a state of awe, fully enamoured by her surroundings. Frogs and crabs, a multitude of insects, little white ones with a fantail, which turned out to be a type of aphid. Another day on the comely beach, whiled away a perfectly languid period of time, the backdrop green and leafy, the sea intoxicatingly warm.

While we were sipping our morning tea, a medium sized reptile was climbing the tree in front of us. Ally decided to get a photo, and approached cautiously to take the picture. Suddenly, a much larger iguana exploded away from behind the tree, sending Ally reeling back in a panic. Funny as fuck. We went to Uvita, knowing she would also love it there, and I'd made a booking at the Toucan hostel that I'd checked out when last there. Simply sublime surroundings. We hiked to a nearby waterfall, with a swimming pool beneath; taking a cooling dip, Ally's hands unexpectedly started to swell up, going from the heat to the cold quickly I suppose. Luckily it went down almost immediately, we were quite a way from town, so could have become serious. On the way back, two guys were bringing together two horses for mating purposes. We had to stop and watch as they were doing it right in the middle of the track. Mildly erotic in a bizarre sort of way, the stalion neighed loudly on his vinegar stroke, and the guys said to us, not a bad occupation hey? Jack was the proprietor of the hotel, and they served good food, beer and wine, so that was our evening sorted.

Spent the day in the bewitching marine park, snorkelling and hiking through the forest. Ally is a nature lover also, so she was deeply impressed with what she was seeing, so much life, very little human interference, the nature just allowed to be; there is no need of management by us. We booked onto the dolphin watching tour for tomorrow, and relaxed away the evening at the hostel, a few others about to chat with, Jack's hospitality and fine fare made everything exemplary. Knowing you are in some sort of pristine environment really gives you a feel good sensation.

A quiet morning, just chilling with all the activity in the gardens, views of the gorgeous coastline, flowers and dense vegetation, a multitude of beautiful birds. Couldn't connect to the internet to check mail, but not bothered, it wasn't such a big deal then, as it seems to be now. Arvo out on a boat, a resident pod of Pacific or pantropical spotted dolphins the highlight of the day. They were threatened at one time during the 80s, with very bad tuna fishing practises, but the industry was forced to change its ways, and their numbers slowly increased. Rays jumping out of the sea often, the shoreline rugged, with a series of caves and arches formed by wind and water erosion over millions of years. A floating log occupied by six brown boobies with yellow feet resting upon it. They dive for fish especially when a predator below, sharks or dolphins, are pushing them towards the surface. Gotta say, there's nothing quite like viewing three pairs of brown boobies!

Got up to catch the 5am bus to Ciudad Cortés then another to Palmar Norte, and a third to Sierpe, relieved that all was going smoothly with the public transport whilst I've got Ally with me. At the jetty, the boat to Bahia Drake was readying for departure, and had space for us, perfect timing. A stunning ride down the serpentine river system and out into the estuary, jungle settings surrounding us, macaws flying across the watery divide between the two banks. Didn't quite get my landing onto the beach right, and seawater washed over my shoes, making them wet. Alex, the boat captain gave us directions to our intended digs, sloshing there with our packs, to find another exquisite location, with beautiful natural grounds, and saw immediately toucans, macaws and hummingbirds, plus hordes of other avians as time went by. When we went to eat, an Alaskan couple invited us to join them, and shared their fish that they had caught themselves, we just had to buy veggies and drinks. A great couple of hours spent with them, and the essential torch we'd brought helped us home, enjoying a bottle of vino on the veranda before retiring. Another impeccable day.

Luis, our skipper and guide for the day came to seek us out when we were finishing up our morning meal. Another group on the boat got dropped off at a beach, then we moored up near San Pedrillo ranger station, which was back in Corcovado National park. A decent hike through the luxuriant tropical forest of oh so many different species of flora from the canopy to the understory, shrub layer and undergrowth. Strangler figs, like thick cobwebs, overwhelmed some trees, a remarkable addition to the evolutionary story. We saw white faced monkeys, Luis knew where some lived, the great advantage of hiring an escort. Also a solitary howler monkey, tiger herons in a nest with chicks and an indigo snake native to Costa Rica, non venomous, and it allowed us a good look at it. Lunch in the bush, then to a waterfall, a refreshing cool off, another smaller snake, maybe a vine, skittered across the river nearby. A bit of a burn off for me, Ally still a bit cautious, but her colour is coming along nicely. Tried to organise some diving for tomorrow, but some uncertainty as yet to whether it is on, numbers again presumably. A pleasant evening in our new local, the torch for navigating back indispensable.

I went to check if it was on, they were all a bit vague, uncommunicative, but we are going, so selected some gear and went back to fetch Ally. The first at Arches, Isla del Caño, had an aquarium feel to it, lots of white tip reef sharks quite active. Small shoals of blue finned tuna and snappers, plenty of pufferfish including guineafowl, and a few groupers. Not a lot of corals, but many small sea fans. Ally had enjoyed her snorkelling, she hadn't fancied diving, sort of out of practise, and couldn't be bothered with a refresher course. An hour and half on the beach, having a snack and cold drinks, saw Luis from yesterday for a chat. El barco hundido, our second dive, wasn't a wreck as the name would suggest. An excellent hour though, more white tips, moray eels, garden eels, big shoals of snapper and grunts, titan triggerfish, porkfish, stingrays and drumfish. My fix gotten, feeling good as usual, which made the journey back seem tranquil, that sense of serenity rippled through the ether. We had a nice snapper dinner at our new favourite eatery, lovely and fresh, few beers, and our now obligatory shared bottle on the veranda. Ally was a good conversationalist, we covered a lot of topics, she was interested in new ideas, and embraced some of the things I'd been discovering, global affairs, environmental issues and why the world is the way it is.

Time to head back to San José, get a car and explore other places. We met up with Alex for the pre arranged boat ride back to Sierpe, more splendor en route. Breakfast at a nice cafe, then a colectivo to Palmar Norte, and a bus to San Isidro, me having to stand most of the way. That took a while, so we will stay overnight there and continue tomorrow. We got a twin at the Astoria with a private bathroom and tv. Found the post office to buy stamps for postcards, then tried again to do mail, but yet another crappy connection, and give it up once more. Relaxed for a bit, watching a bit of news on the tele. Shower, and out for a feed and a few, continuing our chat about all manner of stuff.

We hadn't realised it was Semana Santa, or Easter, it was only Thursday, but everything was closed because of the celebration. McDonalds was open funnily enough so had to have a rubbish breaky there. Were the buses running? Yes, luckily, so a three hour ride back to the capital through some cloud forest, and to a more cooler and comfortable altitude of over 1000 metres. We agreed a price with a taxi driver, and got in. Then some others came over to talk to him, offering a higher fare, so he kicked us out. Got another to Tranquillo, getting a twin again, and went to secure a car, no problem, will collect it tomorrow. I gave Ally a guided tour of SJ, hitting the ATM on the way. She quite liked the city, It's fine, not particularly dangerous like other Central American metropolises. Also, it's clean, the people are mostly friendly, and it has some decent colonial buildings, and places to sit though most were shut now. Getting beer was problematic, and we discovered that Costa Rica practises two dry days for Easter! Fucking hell! It seemed that the posh hotels were exempt, so we ate at one, a lady playing the piano for a pleasing background harmony, and our beer was served in plastic cups for some reason? Maybe they weren't strictly allowed to sell alcohol? Someone had smuggled a stash into the hostel, so we paid for some, and chatted to the others, including Irish David who I'd encountered before.

Brought Ally a cuppa to the room, and went to organise a pancake breakfast. I waited in the lobby to get picked up by the car rental guy, and to the office to do the paperwork. It had a tape player, so dug out my cassettes to listen to on the jaunt to Monteverde. There was a main road most of the way, but the track up to Monteverde itself was in awful condition, and had to drive very slowly, which took an age. We asked the question at a hotel with a restaurant, and they said they would be serving beer and wine in the evening, so we checked in there, booking the nighttime forest tour also through them. Big performance buying ciggies, most shops were shut, it was Good Friday, but found a little stall open in the end. Bit of research on the canopy skywalk for tomorrow, all too easy it seemed.

After sunset, we spent a couple of hours in a rather large group, with Adrian as our guide, quietly walking through the forest with torches. Adrian was excellent, he knew everything about the animals, plants and insects that we saw; lots and lots. We learnt so much about click beetles, stick insects, walking sticks, cicadas, a myriad of other colourful beetles. A tarantula, fireflies, moths, tiny tree frogs, sleeping birds in the boughs, a rare salamander, a kinkajou and a two toed sloth high up in the canopy. It was truly wonderful, a very special experience, seeing all that at nightime, like on the coral reefs, different activities occur when it's dark. A strangler vine that had encompassed a tree, and put down roots, crushing its victim slowly over decades, the poor ceiba, Adrian reckoned, eventually dying and decomposing. We could look up the empty interior of the vine's new space, where other flora, mosses etc, took root also. Absolutely fascinating; nature is bizarre and awe inspiring. All the aliens you ever need are right here on Earth. They didn't seem to give a fuck about the alcohol prohibition, so we got beer and wine with our meal; we bought a round for the staff as a tip, as we were thankful. Wildlife even in our room, in the form of moths and beetles.

There were no curtains at the windows, so we got woken at first light. Some chores, like laundry and Ally was keen to do some shopping, lots of trinkety and arty type retail outlets, that were now all open again. In the afternoon, we drove to the famous skywalk entrance, and spent an incredible few hours hiking the trails and hanging bridges. You traverse the walkways at canopy level, with some small clearings where you can see the jungle undergrowth.

It is called The Monteverde Cloud Forest Biological Preserve, and hosts an incredible array of biodiversity, one of the major hotspots in the whole world. So much that I didn't note in my diary, but have recorded a long good look at a resplendent quetzal, which was an animal, a stunning bird, I was longing to view in the wild. Really worth googling images for that one. Time had flown by, and we were struggling with the fact that Ally was in her last couple of days, before returning to the UK. So we had a bit of a sesh that evening.

A casual morning, got fed and drank some tea, loaded the car and checked out. I had decided on a longer more scenic route back to San José, around the shoreline of Lago Arenal, giving Ally some views of perfect cone shaped volcanoes. Was regretting that, driving to Tilarán, as the excuse for a road was diabolical, and could only move at about 20 to 30 kph. I related the whole trip to Ally on the way, again, quite impressed with my memory. A sealed thoroughfare eventually materialised, and we made better progress, and Ally got her panoramas and photos. It is a glorious route, verdant lush vegetation, the striking blue of the water, and those peaks make great pictures. It was Easter Sunday, and parades were out in force, being a very Christian country, so that held us up going through towns. We stopped for lunch in La Fortuna, lack of signs causing some stress, but finally we were on the main drag to the capital city. We went slightly upmarket for her last night, and after a good clean up and change of clothes, we had a smashing shrimp based meal in the restaurant, all the trimmings, with some beers and a bottle of fine wine.

Relish the comparative luxury, no rush, Ally's flight isn't until the early evening. After our last breakfast together for a while, we took our stuff back to the Tranquillo, me renting a bed in the dorm again. I dropped the car back, traffic heavy even though it was still a holiday, then got a lift home. Last bit of shopping for Ally, she found the picture frames she wanted at last. Couple of farewell beers in a local place, then it was time to return her to the airport. After she had checked in, we had a last smoke together outside, both a bit sad, a long hug, then waved as she went back into the terminal, a weight on my heart, but I will see her again in a few short weeks. Back to buses, the budget in a bit of disarray, and will have to go cheap once more. Bit of net time, another quake in Sumatra made me panic, but looks like it was somewhere remote, and not a high death toll like the last one; no tsunami resulted from it either thankfully. There were a few people about, Jo who had been a divemaster in Utila, and a group of Danish lads. Played some backgammon, then the chessboard came out, me being challenged to a game. He was all over me right from the beginning, backpedaling until he mated me; I'm clearly out of practise. Dorm syndrome denied me a great deal of sleep, an alarm clock tick tocking was the main annoyance.

Pancakes. I will do my utmost not to eat pancakes with syrup again for quite some time. Checked mail and news, the quake was a biggy, but not a major event in human costs; there's clearly some plate tectonic shifting underway over in Asia. A nice chat with two guys from bath, a city very near to where I live in the UK. I walked to the bus station to save money, and boarded the one heading for Cahuita, quite a long ride, but sat next to an Irish/Canadian girl living in Switzerland, so had good company. We arrived about 2pm, a rasta guy touted me and led me to Minas guest house, $10, but good and clean. Bit of bathing in the clear sea, and browning up a bit more, some of the sand was black, from volcanic deposits, palm trees lined the beachhead, quite idyllic. I found out that you have to pay $26 departure tax leaving Costa Rica, which was shit as I didn't have enough to cover it, no ATM in Cahuita, it's a small town. Others told me it wasn't the case, but found a restaurant that would give me some cashback on my card just in case. Would have to go back to Limón otherwise. A decent creole feed, getting $30 in hard currency, then home to read and sleep.

Up at 7am, and to the local soda to eat, cafes where the natives dine, reasonable grub, and cheap. A drunk was reciting bus times in Spanish and English, latching on to me to scrounge. Gave him cigarettes to get rid of him, but it didn't work, he followed me around. A local bus to Sixaola, fully in Garifuna territory, a mix of Central American, Caribbean Africans, who have formed their own creole languages and cultures. Through Puerto Viejo, then into Bribri, home to the interesting looking Bribri tribe, where I spotted an ATM! These journeys always take time, lots of stopping and starting, faffing and discussion, but eventually we got to Sixaola, and the border. Stamped out of Costa Rica, no departure tax, so needn't have worried. Cross the bridge over the river of the same name, an old rickety steel structure that was once a railway, easier to step on the sleepers to traverse. Panama immigration was closed for lunch, so had to wait, chatting to the others who were there also. Got stamped into Panama, no tourist card for EU passport holders, fucking bonus. Shared a pick up with some girls, driven by an angry man, to Changuinola, then a colectivo to Finca 63. A boat to Bocas del Toro town, down the river to the sea, and along the beautiful coastline, of mangrove and sandy stretches, all looking totally wild. Many species of seabirds sighted, including pelicans, frigatebirds, gulls and gannets.

Couldn't believe what I was reading when I disembarked the vessel at the boathouse. A notice on the wall, advertising currently needing volunteers to work on a leatherback turtle project. I had thought that I was not going to be there at the right time of year, when nesting takes place, but turns out that it varies, from species to species. I was very excited about it. I went straight to the address, but there was no one to speak to, so I went and checked into a basic hotel, The Emanuel. I was restless with enthusiastic anticipation; what if it was an old poster that someone had forgot to take down? Bit of a walk around, then I couldn't stand it any longer, and returned to the house, where I found Carolina, the program manageress, who told me all the details and costs. I went and got the money, $120 for a week if I recall correctly, and booked my place, and will be heading to Soropta beach tomorrow; I was thrilled. She invited me to join her for dinner, so went and showered, then had a couple of beers, my leg constantly jiggling in motion as I conjured up images of expectation. We ate, conversing continuously about what was involved, and what I would experience. We ended up at the Wreck Deck bar, an open air venue built over the shoreline where a ship had sunk. After a few more, she tried, unsuccessfully, to teach me how to salsa.

Another room with no windows, so it was still dark when I woke up, but about 7am, and light flooded in when I opened the door. Had to do a bit of shopping, so I got something to eat plus tea, then gathered some provisions, collected bags, and went to the boat departure place to meet Carolina. A lovely ride along coastlines of no human presence, mangroves intact by the looks. Through some channels, out into what appeared to be open seas, finally arriving at Soropta. A short distance to the very basic dwellings around a central building which was the hub of the turtle conservation project. I met Ramón and Natalia who were the qualified naturalists or biologists. Clemente, Mau and Raul were indidgenous Americans, whose fathers had been poachers, and they had decided to turn the tide and become protectors of the wildlife, attempting to educate their countrymen of the importance of preservation so as not to render species extinct. Gabriel was a volunteer like myself, and the other lady had finished and was returning to town on the boat I had come on. Damari, the resident cook, was putting the final touches to lunch, so the first thing was to eat, and exchange information about ourselves; loving these people already, so focused on protection of nature.

Got my bed, and shown around, back to primitive living for a week, no electricity, rainwater collection and a simple filter purifier. Toilets of the long drop type, and water for washing had to be drawn from a well. Ducks and chickens for meat and eggs, some veggies and fruit grown on site, and obviously supplies were brought from Bocas del Toro when paying participants were delivered there. No wastefulness, everyone pro conservation, very little plastic, rustic to the extreme; I was in my element. Helped to gather some firewood, not needed for heating but for cooking. The beach was dark coloured, volcanic ash drops again, and driftwood scattered all along it, natural debris from storms, a good source of energy when dried. Relaxed in a hammock reading for a bit, then went to mingle, Natalia giving me the rundown, I was going on my first patrol at 10pm. Cena by candlelight, tried to doze for an hour, then got ready to go, wide awake and buzzing with the possibilities of seeing a turtle laying eggs on a remote and untamed strand.

Soft sand syndrome made for a tough hike along the beach, each step having to pull your foot free of suction. There were some firmer stretches that were a relief for a while. Clemente was our guide, and Gabriel was the third member of our patrol; we had torches with a red film over the beam so as not to dazzle the turtles. After about half an hour, a shape appeared in the near distance, and Clemente declared it to be an egg laying female; my pulse shot up as the brain chemicals exploded into my neural pathways. A quarter of a metric tonne animal, a leatherback turtle, was already poised to start dropping her eggs into the hole that she had dug. I was given a plastic carrier bag which I had to hold open inside the pit to catch the precious deposits, the future of an endangered species. Clemente and Gabriel went a way up the shore to prepare a second burrow, to relocate the priceless cargo into, thus thwarting the poachers who patrol the coast looking out for the furrows made by the turtles as they drag themselves up the sand.

AWESOME, AWESOME, AWESOME. When we had finished, the final task was to brush away our footprints from around the new site, we continued on our way. My happiness was overwhelming me, and I forgot about the discomfort of the trudge. We found another nest, already filled back in, and the mother returned to sea; but we relocated the valuable contents anyway, every egg matters in the desperate conservation program. Suddenly, there was activity again, it was Ramón and Mau, who had left on the 8pm patrol, and were on their way back, but had found another egg laying female to attend to. Apparently, they go into a sort of trance as they drop their clutch, so they are quite oblivious to our presence, as long as we are quiet and are mostly behind them, which the experts amongst us were keen to educate me on. We went to the limit of our stretch of beach, a fair few kilometres from the base, and rested for a spell. Then the hard slog back, not encountering any more reptiles, but a perfect first night for me, and I collapsed into my bed about 3am, exhausted but exhilarated.

It rained a lot during the night, but my enthusiasm spilled over into the next day, and it was all I could converse about. An American called Ann arrived on the first boat, and later, Dawi and Theresa from Holland came to join us for a few days, me constantly rabbiting about last night's experiances. There was a lot of literature about the program, and information about leatherback turtles to digest. They are the biggest of all turtle species, and can weigh up to 700 kilograms. They have been around in their present form for over 100 million years, so swam the oceans when dinosaurs were roaming the landmasses of Earth. Pretty much global distribution, and they travel enormous distances, but females return to the beach that they hatched on to lay their own eggs. Their numbers are in decline in the present day because of human pressures; getting caught up in fishing nets, eating plastic waste that floats on the ocean currents. In the dimness, mistaking it for jellyfish, their natural prey, which clogs up their guts; and poaching of eggs. They are believed to have aphrodisiac properties, which is unfounded in studies. There were posters everywhere, with a turtle holding up a viagra pill, pleading to the population to take them for some extra sex drive rather than our precious ovums. Along with conservation efforts, that included educating the public, the tide was slowly turning in favour of the magnificent animals. Just hope it's not too late.

Natalia was one of the most passionate environmentalists that I ever met. She was from Columbia, and had dedicated her life to the cause, and especially all species of turtles; this was just her present and latest calling, the most recent of dozens of projects that she had been involved with. She could speak quite good English, so our conversations spanned two languages, me keen to keep up with Spanish practise. It stayed cloudy all day, with some spitting rain, but in the tropics, it doesn't really get cold. Small wildlife in the form of amphibians of a myriad species, including tree frogs, birds and insects in prolific numbers; a truly natural wonderland of wildness unsullied by human development. I drew a bucket of water for a wash in the little wooden cubicles, and joined the others for dinner. I was going to be on a much later patrol, so got a couple more hours of sleep during the evening, and set off with Ramón, Raul and Ann after midnight, the darkness complete, as it remained overcast. A finished nest early on, but the tide was coming in, and erasing the ruts, so we decided to leave it be. The sand was firmer, so seemed easier to walk, and it ended up being a quiet shift, none of the patrols found any laying females that whole night, and I fell gratefully into bed about 5am. Ramón, a biologist from Spain, was also very dedicated and extremely knowledgeable about the animals we were there to protect, and so much more; a fascinating guy to have social intercourse with. A few people went to Changuinola for supplies, some just for the ride, so I relaxed with my book, and more turtle literature. After lunch, when everyone was back, we played cards and dice, then a volleyball game on the beach, a lovely sunny day. I was designated for the later patrol again, so after dinner and a wash, I grabbed a bit more shut-eye. Me, Ann, Raul and Mauricio, a local from a nearby village who came and went as needed, set off about midnight, the lack of a rising moon made the darkness absolute except for the beautiful clear starry night sky brimming with distant suns. Ann tripped at one point, on some driftwood, and grazed her shin, so I was helping her along, but my feet got wet from the incoming tide. Just makes the hike more uncomfortable, and unfortunately, caused a blister on one of my heels, adding to the discomfort. We rested at post 80, and a shooting star shot through the heavens, which gave me hope, seeing it as providence, an omen that we were going to find a turtle on our return. Alas, it wasn't to be; I felt so sorry for Ann, who hadn't seen one yet, and wanted her to share my elation. Teas and fags whilst tending to the new wound, it was quite bad, but sleep was beckoning, and I crashed and burnt for a good catch up kip.

I borrowed some flip flops, my sandal straps rubbed on the blister, and I wanted to air it throughout the day. Some interaction with the chicks and ducklings, everyone talking, a real social atmosphere; felt like family. The local men are of the Ngäbe-Buglé comarca, the most populous of Panama's indidginous tribes. They are key to persuading their friends and families to desist with consuming turtle eggs and easing the burden on the conservation effort. Of course, it is an age old tradition, making change in especially older people's behaviour very difficult. The war was being won, very slowly, but surely, as the younger generation understands that when the leatherback is extinct, there will be no more eggs anyway. A disturbing and upsetting thing I heard about was that some hardcore poachers, who refuse to believe that there is a problem, have taken to capturing the animals at sea, cutting them open to get the eggs out of them!!

A laying female was seen by last night's final patrol at post 71, must have come ashore shortly after we had passed by. I taught Dawi how to play backgammon, and we played a few games, then some cards, and the usual lunch, banter, siesta and wash. Strange and vivid dreams, a bit feverish, and wondered if I had malaria again, but told that there is none there. I'd heard that you can suffer flashbacks, so put it down to that, and I had no more incidents thereafter. Shoes dried out, blister patched up, we set off, Dawi, Raul and Mauricio were my fellow sentinels that shift. It was another clear night, the stunning sky a big distraction, but I am getting familiar with certain landmarks now, and learnt where the firmer sand is, to make the going easier. We met the earlier patrol, and they had relocated a nest, Theresa and Ann's first; I was so stoked up for them. Unfortunately, we didn't see one, and on the way back, it clouded over and started to drizzle. We got back before the worst of it, got the kettle on the stove and knocked up a brew before crashing again, falling into the new pattern of existence.

The girls had been on a nature walk, and were raving about the wildlife they had seen, especially copious numbers of butterflies. Theresa was leaving, so we all fussed around her, and waved our farewells as the boat disappeared from view. A storm was brewing, so we spent a lot of the afternoon in the dining area, playing cards, chatting and joking; I really liked this group of people, nature lovers, intelligent and fun. There were tee shirts for sale and candle holders made from bamboo; I bought one of the shirts, obviously turtle themed. Everybody loved my Australian aboriginal art tee shirt, it had a kangaroo print on the front: I decided to donate it to someone, but who? We came up with a game involving cards, and Raul won it, but Natalia offered him hard cash for it, so it ended up belonging to her.

I got allocated to the early shift, the climate was pretty filthy, but we got some wet weather gear to wear. We whiled away some time, no one very enthusiastic about braving the storm. Clemente, who's nickname had become OJ, due to the fact that he consumed large quantities of orange juice, was teaching Dawi how to salsa. Well, there's no more excuses, we've got to go, it's going to be unpleasant, but there's work to be undertaken. It was pitch black, the sky completely dark, heavy with dense clouds, the contents of being deposited upon us, and whipped into our faces by the wind. We got a turtle at post 77, the first for Dawi. She was covering the nest again having presumably laid her clutch into it. A beautiful wildlife scene as she finished up and dragged herself back to the angry sea, disappearing into the surf, her exhausting efforts accomplished. It was decided to leave it alone, the location marked in a log, to be monitored, but the furrows mother turtle had made were already being eliminated by the rain and surge. We doubted any poachers would be active, as they usually came along the shoreline in small boats, but the storm would most likely make it too hazardous that night. One thing that annoyed me was that we had been told that photography wasn't allowed, the camera flash would spook the turtles. Dawi had taken some photos with a red film over the flashbulb, so had gotten permission to do so? Why? By the time we were on the return leg, I was utterly drenched, so I just walked in the frothy shallows where the sand was a tad firmer.

There was going to be a change of some of the staff, so most people went in the boat for a visit to town. I was quite happy to stay put, I would be returning in a couple of days' time anyway, and was enjoying the remoteness, away from civilization. So me and OJ chatted and drank tea, well me, he stuck to his favored juice. A spell in the hammock reading, the weather was still shitty and it was going to be difficult to dry everything out ready for the night shift. The kitchen and dining area had wet clothes and shoes all over, and the heating was on to help the evaporation of dampness from the garments and footwear. The vessel returned and I was introduced to David, Emilio and Odilia who was the new cook. I went to the toilet, they were proper bowls, with seats perched above a long drop that you had to put compost into to keep the smell at bay. There was a snake coiled up behind the throne, so I used the next one and informed everyone about it. They came to look and said it was non venomous, a bird eater, so we just left it be, it would go out again when it got hungry: I do love snakes, an evolutionary success story and that element of extreme danger.

Rain, rain and more rain, the air thick with humidity, the moistness keeping all of the clothes dank, and we had run out of dry firewood. The others came back about five ish with tales of town, as if it was some mythical place of legends. They had treats though, so we all got stuck into them. Natalia said she couldn't get me cigarettes, which caused my heart to sink, but she was teasing me in the end, payback for the trick I played on her yesterday. After dinner, we were assigned our patrol stints, and I got the final one of the night, not starting until 4am. I went to bed, but was suddenly being called by Natalia, and thought I had overslept, but there was a laying turtle right in front of the settlement, and she decided, rightfully, that I would want to view it. Such a wonderful sight, I was very happy, and so glad that this opportunity had presented itself to me. That week in Soropta is still one of the highlights of my entire life.

Quick cup of tea as we are putting on damp clothing, but it was raining still, so not really worth donning dry garb, will save it for our return. Just me and Natalia set out, Ann was feeling a bit crook, so stayed in bed. It was pitch black, the weak torchlight barely breaking a metre into the gloom, so had to tread carefully, and watch out for driftwood. We met Ramón and co about half way, them on the reciprocal homeward bound leg. They had not encountered any turtles, but we continued to the end of our stretch, the precipitation sometimes torrential. Natalia was a fascinating human being to chat with, she had done so much good in this sometimes disheartening world, completely selfless, only interested in the salvation of wildlife and nature. A truly beautiful soul, and immensely knowledgeable, and she seemed to like me and value my thoughts and ideas. A staunch conservationist, if only a few percent of humanity were as like minded as Natalia, the planet would be an infinitely better place.

It became dawn, and I saw for the first time how it all looked in daylight, a wild and untamed location of outstanding pulchritude. We didn't expect to find turtles now, so picked up the pace and continued to converse, I really loved being in her company. We attempted to hike the nature trail, but it was pissing down, and pools of water underfoot, though my feet and shoes were already saturated; but we didn't see anything, it was all sheltering from the elements. Grab some dry gear, and peel off the wet stuff, wringing it out and hanging it up again, little hope of it drying out unless this bugger of a weather front finally passes over. Tea and breakfast were being prepared, and I gratefully consumed my share, then to bed for a bit of catch up sleep.

I was awoken for lunch, and guess what? Yes, it was still raining, it seemed half the Caribbean sea had been deposited upon us. An afternoon of cards, backgammon and chat, the fire spitted constantly, as the fuel was damp, but some meagre heat was radiated out into the room, and the clothing was partially dry at least. Ann was fretting about a nest that may have been poached, it was going to happen occasionally; our job was to minimise the losses. Dinner, and I'm on the midnight shift, so try to get another hour's sleep, but not really tired, so more of a doze. Go get some tea before setting off, Natalia is ill now, probably all the damp weather, so I will patrol with Ramón. The rain finally started to ease, but no stars to be seen, so we put our wet weather gear on just in case. The sand was softer than usual so it was a trudge, and got hot, so had to carry the waterproofs, the drizzle petering out at last. We came upon the earlier unit working at relocating a nest at post 58, so helped them to finish up, and that turned out to be my last sighting; not too bad methinks, five in the week, so I was happy enough, and fond memories are forefront in my mind as I type these words in early 2021. Ramón produced a cigarette and a match plus some strike at our rest stop, as it was my last night on the project. It wasn't allowed to smoke on the beach normally, but they made an exception for me, and I obviously kept the butt in my pocket until we got home. The rain stayed off except for a bit of mizzle, and was relieved to be back at base, the going had been a bit torturous, and gratefully got the kettle on the hob for a brew, before retiring into a deep sleep.

It was late morning when I surfaced, Ann had left on the early boat, but we'd said goodbyes yesterday. We ate a scant lunch, Natalia and Ramón were returning to Bocas with me, raving about a burger restaurant that they were going to take me to, where we would say our farewells, though we would keep in touch via email. Nick was a new volunteer, who'd come on the vessel that picked up Ann, so I chatted with him whilst we waited, excitedly giving him all the details of my week there. Everyone came to the jetty, but the craft just sped by! Natalia was furious, she really was looking forward to that burger it seemed. She phoned up base in town, there was a mobile phone on site in case of emergencies, and got some feeble excuse; the next wasn't until 4.30pm. It rained more, then stopped, so we got a photoshoot done, OJ making tracks in the sand as a turtle would, laughing at the possibility of fooling poachers.

The next boat was an hour late, and the piss taking began about us having to forego that juicy cheeseburger, those crispy fries, and, Ooohhh, the cold beer. I hadn't realised how much I was looking forward to my first jar of amber nectar in over a week.

Eventually, it parked up, and we were on our way, waving to our companions, people who seemed to me now more like brothers and sisters. A close knit community, in a remote setting, with common goals, and the need for everyone to be proactive in the well being or basically, survival of everybody else does that to your psyche; strong emotional bonds are formed, and it gave me insight into how our species got to where it is, knowing for most of our history, we had been tribes and clans of hunter gatherers or foragers. Trust amongst the band, affinity, kinship, cooperation and of course, love, are all important elements for the success of the whole. Another stunning journey up river back to the city, or so it seemed to me; civilization, lots of people, development and the progress of humanity, which I sometimes question deeply. We could stay at Carolina's, she had quite a large property assigned to her to be able to do her job, mattresses on the floors in the bedrooms, absolutely fine. I met Suelaker, a Mexican chica, who was going out to Soropta tomorrow. Chat a lot, and get a shower, then for the grand finale, which didn't disappoint, big juicy burgers and chips, and that first coldie was like ecstasy. To the wreck deck afterwards for a semi session, drinking and dancing. Back at Carolina's, me and Suelaker sat out on the veranda, with a little un, and talked into the night, her speaking English and me speaking Spanish.

Rudely awoken early, but a nice cuppa was delivered into my hands. The rest of them, except Natalia, were heading to the project, so I said goodbyes all round and went to check into a slightly upmarket hotel. The most desperate task was to get laundry in to be washed, and when that was done, I went to find breakfast. I procured an old newspaper, to stuff inside my shoes, helping to get them properly dried, and spent a couple hours online, sending block emails as I had a lot to tell. The main news of the day was the pope's funeral taking place. Shaved off a week's growth, and was about to siesta when I got a message from Natalia to meet up for lunch. She was truly excellent company, and it ended up being over two hours, with some food and three beers. I was really tired now, the drink had made me sleepy, and after hugging our final farewells, I went back to the hotel to crash. And that was that until the early hours of the next day, a proper good catch up slumber.

Feeling fully refreshed, I got out early to eat a morning meal, pretty hungry by then. Collected my clean, dried and pressed garments, a pleasurable extravagance when backpacking in the wet tropics. It was raining hard again, the cheap brolley getting lots of use; at least my boots were nearly fully dehydrated. Packed up, and waited for a break in the weather, then quickly walked to the boat where there were regular crossings back to Almirante. I got a taxi to the bus terminal, and spent a pleasant four hours traversing the Panamanian isthmus to the second largest city by population, David. Through forest reserves and tropical panoramas, all lush and green after the copious amount of rainfall recently deposited on the landscape. I found my way eventually, using Lonely Planet's rubbish maps, to Pension Klark. Quite often a landmark is recorded on the street plan, on the wrong side of the road; which has you going in the incorrect direction! Fucking infuriating.

It was a nice room, but a bit more expensive than quoted in LP. Nearly all private rooms throughout Central America have tvs in them, which is good for listening to Spanish, but the best of it is the 'movie' channel. I spent some time trying to formulate a plan. I had about three weeks left before my flight from New York departed back to London, and was aware that I would need to buy a connection from Panama city probably, to get back there. But for now, I wanted one last adventure, and the cities weren't going to satisfy my lust. The Darién region interested me, but sounded pretty rough there, full of narco traffickers and a bit wild westy. The city of David was unremarkable, not saying it's not worth visiting, but there are better examples of colonial architecture elsewhere. It was pleasant enough, cheap places to sit and drink a couple of beers, and eat a meal. The people were friendly, I was told parts of the Darién were okay to visit, and jungle hiking should be available, but don't go anywhere near the Darién gap!

I went to eat at the bus station, so I could buy a ticket to Santiago de Veraguas for later. Another picturesque ride through tropical landscapes, I never seem to tire of such journeys, I just feel at peace passing through places, gazing out of the window, always something of interest to view. Rolling forest covered hills, and a lot more agricultural land, though it still seemed organic, and nature was given her space to continue to thrive. I was only going to overnight there, so I just paid $23 for the smart hotel near the terminal, with tv, baño privado y piscina, or a swimming pool in the grounds. Santiago was a little bit more elegant than David, a nice cathedral and central plaza. Couple hours by the pool, last chances of topping up the tan perhaps? There were geese roaming the grounds, and quite a lot of bird life in the shrubbery. A bar next door served cold beer, and nearby places to eat, but I had a quiet one, ending up watching a film: and some 'movies.'

The next leg to Panama city was a bit disappointing, so much more farmland, I suppose to feed the population of the capital and the numerous smaller centres of humanity that have sprung up around the canal region. It's ugly to me, urban sprawls, roads, cultivated earth, regimentally planted trees for paper pulp, the few protected areas mostly secondary forest; all of which seem to be becoming the norm across the planet. You could see the high-rise of the central business district from quite a way out, and as we entered the conurbation, there were row after row of shabby blocks of apartments. The bus terminated at Allbrook, and found the local transport to España, roughly where I had chosen a hostel to check out. Street name signs seemed to be in short supply, which made navigating with the shit LP map frustrating: and asking people sent me back and forth, as most would just tell you anything, afraid to admit they simply didn't know! Eventually, I homed in on the Voyager hostel, which was fine, so I paid for a bed in a dorm.

Got chatting to an Irish chap called Neil, loved that aspect of hosteling, you would just meet people straight away, and everybody who stayed in them was after the same thing; social interaction. Alas, that doesn't seem to be the case anymore; hostel common rooms have become places where people sit around staring at a screen! I did a quick bit of email, there were some issues to do with the rent from the house, but Gina was on it. Got me thinking about what to do, and just determined to wait until I got home, and had spoken to Gina about what she had decided. I met a guy called Barrie, who was a boat skipper, and trying to find passengers to take to Columbia via the San Blas islands, a common route, as only the extremly brave or the incredibly stupid attempted to go through the Darién gap. I told him I was at the end of my trip, and would be returning home shortly, but he was very persistent, to the point of becoming rather bothersome. Jimmy's rest over the road for food and a couple of bevvies. The hostel bar had sold out, so I had to go to the supermarket. The kitchen fridge stated that it wasn't allowed to keep alcoholic drinks in there! Well, they should keep the bar stocked then shouldn't they? I squeezed it in amongst the food, and got talking to a fellow countryman from Plymouth. He had travelled a lot; a hell of a lot it became apparent, and a nice evening unfolded.

The free breakfast provided by the hostel wasn't great, cheap bread and the most economical, second rate, inferior axle grease, which claimed to be margarine on the tub, that you can imagine. I wanted to visit Panama Viejo, so I paid another night, and started to walk in that direction, stopping to check out costs of flights back to the USA en route. Bit shocking, cheapest was $450! Early lunch in a local, I couldn't eat much of the crap offerings this morning. Then an engaging few hours wandering the ruins of the old and original city which has a rich and quite violent history. Again, go to images on google. It is situated right on the Pacific coast, and there was also a lot of information about the local ecology, the mangroves and the mud flats that were visible to me. It was all protected, and certainly looked to have a healthy seabird population, but so much more small life existed in profusion. On the way back, I saw an advertisement for a flight to DC for $309, but after taxes etc, it came in at $459! Read and chatted with others staying there, lots of people were doing the San Blas trip to Columbia; I was envious of course, but I couldn't sensibly justify it. I was already thinking about a South America trip maybe next year. A Dutch guy was trying to hire a crew to get his vessel back to Oz; what a dream that would have been. A shower, quick feed and an agreeable few twilight hours on the balcony with beers, a toke and my travelling peers.

Just tea for breakfast, will get something outside, can't eat any of that muck this morning; pay for another night. A bus to Cinco de Mayo, and look around for the transport to the canal locks. People just tell you anything when you ask for directions, but eventually find the one going to Paraiso Ancón which passed close to Miraflores visitor centre, the main set of 'steps' on the great feat of engineering that is The Panama Canal. I pretty much spent the whole day there, it was fascinating reading about how this project was undertaken and all of the problems encountered. The death toll was high as is usually the case with large scale infrastructure builds pre any meaningful human rights laws were operational, a huge mortality rate from malaria for instance. This was all taking place in the early 20th century, and the waterway finally opened to shipping around 1914.

I bought some food, and sat overlooking one of the locks and just watched all the massive cargo vessels going through, one after the other. I attempted to count how many containers were on each colossal freighter, and failed, probably thousands on each one. It is a two way facility, a great manmade lake for ships to pass by each other upstream. Behemoths of oil tankers, and the odd yacht hitchhiking on the back end of the enormous floating fortress, like an oxpecker on an elephant's arse. Most were Chinese judging by the writing on the sides of them, and came to a realisation that all those goods, whatever it was, were coming from China's ports, and this was only what was being delivered to America's eastern seaboard and Europe. There would be much more heading to other parts of Asia, Africa and the western coast of the US and South America that wouldn't need to come through this narrow cutting. Maybe it's a particularly busy day? I mentioned that to the guy on the way out, but he just said, no, that was a bog standard day, not any busier than usual! My God, we, us humans, get through some stuff ongoing, no wonder the planet is choking on our waste! It was a real eye opener for me, the sheer scale of our rampant consumption!

Back in town, I had a wander around the charming Casco Antiguo part of the city, with a nice cathedral, but a lot of the buildings were in a state of disrepair; needed a good old fashioned face lift. It was interesting, and pleasant little local cafes to eat at and sup a coldie. Definitely seemed a much poorer area generally. I picked up a six pack before returning to the hostel for a shower and another evening with the crowd there. The Dutch guy had had some success with crew members for his voyage across the Pacific. New arrivals were an English chap who had worked with a macaw project in Costa Rica, an American who was studying ecology, and an Israeli fellow. The conversation was absorbing enough, as is normally the case with a group of travellers in hostels, most are extroverted. But the subject matter focused around environmental problems facing our species, and the conclusion was, if we continue on our current trajectory, that the future is not very bright or hopeful. The agreed opinion in the wrapping up of the debate was that a different path needed to be found by humanity, a more inclusive and green economy. That would be determined by the governments and big business, so we also reckoned that it was still a long way off, and would probably need a shockwave to bring it about. Not enough people were waking up to the ever pressing issues.

I met a guy called Carlos, who was nice and could speak good English, and said he would help me get a cheap flight to the US. You cannot go through your whole life without trusting absolutely no one, so I was wary, and only gave him a small deposit to secure the ticket but he ripped me off. He had got me a gram of ching though, so not all bad. I got my teeth cleaned at a dentist, so much cheaper than in the UK. It was the start of a weekend, so the hostel filled up, and a good crowd gathered out on the balcony, and a session was on the cards. I had eaten earlier, so settled in to it, a bit of candy already installed onto the mucus membrane. I remet Nick and Pete who I had spent time with in San José; also new arrivals were Lars from Norway and Sven, a cop from East Berlin. They were all up for a bit of charlie, so a full on raucous bender developed and persisted into the hours of the next morning.

Panama is the first port of call for the trade in the white powder that is mostly produced in Columbia, and trafficked through the Darién gap; that's why it is so dangerous to attempt to hike to the neighbouring country via this route, if you meet the narcos, they would rather just dispose of you in case you report seeing them later. So snow is readily available, and cheap. And that was the theme of the weekend, which drifted into the following week. Some people left, but others checked in, so the hostel was buzzing, and partying was on everyone's mind. We became nocturnal, sleeping all day and gathering in the late afternoon, and out on the town all night. Rasputin's was a favourite, and Unplugged for live music and shooting pool. We usually ended up at someone's house to continue until dawn. I almost fucked up, going back with a guy on my own, thinking it was just for drinks and more drugs, but he was gay and wanted to sleep with me. Could have had a very different outcome. I wandered the streets afterwards, not knowing where I was, and no money left in my pockets. No fags also, so had to scronge a couple, and eventually, just got a taxi back to the hostel, shot in to get cash, and paid the driver, before crashing at about 7am.

Another couple of days of that, and I was starting to feel burn-out. An all nighter resulted in an all day sleep, waking in the late afternoon, and deciding enough. Went to get a good meal, as I had not ate properly for several days, then a quieter affair with just a few on the balcony with some Swedes, Germans and an American Taiwanese guy. I couldn't sleep, as my body clock was all out of sync, and was tired in the morning, but had to leave, just needed to get away. I put up with the rubbish breakfast, said a round of goodbyes, and got a taxi to the terminal. The bus took ages to leave, I am on roads less travelled now, only locals it seemed were taking this route. The music was loud, the suspension was crap, and the highway wasn't what you might describe as brilliant. So I got down in Chepo, only about 60 kilometres further towards Darién. A nearby pension was okay, so I got a room there, a quick feed of chow mein, a couple of beers, caught up with some hygiene chores, and a spell in the internet cafe, frustrated by the usual snail's pace of the connection in these rural settings.

There was no one about, so I filled my water bottle from the Igloo and left; I'd already paid. A crummy breakfast at the station, there was a colectivo filling up, and I jumped onto that as it was heading east; it actually departed before it was full! More agriculture dominated landscapes and a large body of water was lake Bayano, which was picturesque. Police checkpoints became common as we neared Darién, just formalities, I had to show my passport, and the cops were friendly towards me. The transport terminated somewhere, and there was a bus going to Meteti, which was my target destination. I bought a ticket, then a long wait, but finally we got underway, but the roads were in pretty shocking condition, so it took an age to complete the journey. A gaggle of kids got on for a spell, writing graffiti on the windows, and generally being a nuisance. The panoramas didn't improve, still predominantly farmland, and deforestation was in top gear, the distant hills already cleared: I might be a decade too late.

The Felicidad hotel was okay, so I rented a room, then walked to town, stupidly forgetting my document! So I had to go back, when a stern, unfriendly policeman demanded that I should always carry it with me. There were lots of Chinese people, and I wondered if that was why the high rate of clearing of the jungle was underway. The Chinese authorities have a habit of doing deals with foreign governments, to build infrastructure in exchange for harvesting the resources. I found the ANAM office, which is Panama's national wildlife directive, and managed to organise a hike into virgin forest for tomorrow morning. Great, sorted, not a waste of time coming all this way after all. There wasn't much about the town, a wild west sort of place, scruffy and worn, people seemed sullen, and violence lurked beneath the surface I felt; something to do with the highly lucrative drugs trade no doubt. Did the bollocks back at the digs, then it was beer o'clock. I met a guy working for USAID, trying to set up an ecotourism business, but he was up against it, the timber value outweighed any long term financial benefits of bringing in sightseers, to view nature; just hoped he wasn't too late! He told me that the whole region is being ravaged by chainsaws, which was depressing to hear; just another nail in nature's coffin, ultimately in ours most likely?

I got a half decent breaky at the hotel restaurant, then wandered along to ANAM's local headquarters. I chatted with the staff there, then a guy pulled up on a motorcycle. And we were away, me riding as a pillion on a trial bike to the start of the trail. A few hours of wonder unfolded, a very good walk through primary forest on a large circular hiking pathway, with tree roots to step over constantly. I'd been told to carry plenty of water, and it was indeed a lot of tough uphill trekking, in very humid conditions, so I was sweating buckets, and needed regular rehydration stops. We had high energy snacks between us, so something to munch on also. You just know when a piece of jungle is uncut, it's well established, the trunks ginormous, vines everywhere and all the other ingredients of old growth forest are present; ferns, mosses, bromeliads, exotic looking flowers, displaying highly sexual stamens and pistils, in dizzying numbers. The canopy was dense and complete, making it quite dark on the ground, and the undergrowth wasn't thick, further substantiating that I was viewing something undisturbed for centuries.

A great indicator of a healthy ecosystem are insects. In the tropics, there are lots of biting ones, so dabs of deet based repellent was essential. The plethora of species that I saw on that ramble was remarkable, and realised that I might be observing critters unknown to science, though I would never be aware of it. It dawned on me that with all the raping and pillaging of the surrounding areas, that there would be a fair few small plants and especially invertebrates, that would become extinct without ever being known to humankind! Very sad, so much medicine is derived from such places, and on the high ground, you could hear the distant brum brumming of powered saws plundering the habitat: a resonance that grated to my very bone marrow. I was in a relatively small domain that was protected for now, but if the right amount of cash greased the right someone's palm? We saw howler and white faced monkeys, anteaters, toucans, hummingbirds and lots of butterflies including blue morpho in abundance, a beautiful sight. little green and black tree frogs, and the pièce de résistance, a rare harpy eagle, huge in the treetops. A hard descent, steep and the track was treacherous with roots, stones and some slippery mud, then the casual ride back to town: mixed feelings engulfed me, elation at what I had been privy to, and despair, knowing it probably wouldn't be there in the not too distant future! Near the soda across the road from my hotel, there was a big parking area for trucks. All the trailers were flat beds, and their cargos were massive tree trunks, some so gigantic, that only one occupied a single rig!!

The return journey was long, as the highway was in poor condition, improving slightly after a certain point. Police checkpoints galore, I had my passport held in my hand for a chunk of the way, as I had to show it so often. Then, suddenly, we were gathering a head of steam, the stops became minimal, and we started into the outskirts of the city. The first sign I saw that read Tocumen, I stopped the bus and jumped down, spotting a pension which was fine and checked into it, $20 for a nice air con room. Tocumen was and probably still is the district where the international airport is located. I got a local transport there, and went in, searching for the American Airlines desk. I bought a flight to JFK, via Miami for a couple days time, and it was only $358 including all taxes. It would mean that I would have to spend four nights in New York. I managed to reconfirm my homeward bound to London whilst I was at it. A quiet evening, a small meal in a local cafe, washed down with a couple of coldies. The complete round of hygiene chores, and a bit of pampering as the room was so pleasant, even an exfoliating foot scrubber in the shower. I settled down to watch some tv, sipping on the bottles I'd bought from a shop. Low and behold, a 'movie' channel, which made the cost of the accommodation seem like great value.

I was rudely awoken by workmen digging up the road outside with pneumatic drills. The general area was not a tourist place, and I doubted that I would be able to entertain myself around here for two more days. I decided to go back to central Panama city, and have a last binge with some travellers in a backpackers. The crowded bus wound into the city, I could see the high rise, but it sort of skirted to the north of the metropolis. I ended up having to get a taxi to the Voyager hostel, and rented a bed in the dorm. One last chore to perform, getting my dirty clothing laundered. So, that was the blowout that ended this trip, or so I thought; a couple of nights getting on it with a crowd of party animals that were staying there, no names recorded unfortunately. But I'm glad that I came back, no one from the previous stay, but nomads from that era knew how to have fun, a lot of laughing and grinning occurred.

My journal becomes a mess of rushed scribbles for the final days of this travel experience, some of the words barely intelligible, and photography ground to a halt. So I'm dredging the brain's vaults, trying to assimilate my memories with the few phrases I've jotted down. Security was going to be tedious ongoing after 9/11, so it was always a good idea to arrive at the airport early. There were no smoking rooms around the departure gate area, so I asked a lady cleaner, and she kept saying baño in a brusque voice, waving her arm in a direction. I thought she was telling me off, until I twigged her meaning, and I went for a crafty one in the toilet cubicle. About three and a half hours later after take off, we put wheels down in Miami. This was where I was puzzled, as it seemed very easy to transfer to the next gate; bearing in mind that I had arrived from outside of the states, I didn't encounter any immigration! Rather odd. It was nearly as far again from Miami to JFK, where there was more scrutiny, and I can't remember if I had to get a new visa waiver, but I was through, and heading into the city on a train.

There was a guy further down the carriage, scruffily dressed and with a rucksack; I hate to prejudicate, but he looked English. I walked past, and said hi, and he answered in a Liverpudlian accent; he was indeed a scouser, therefore, arguably English. He introduced himself as Dennis, and he was going to stay at a hostel in central NY, and invited me to come with him. We hit it off, a similar sense of humour, and we chatted until the train pulled into Penn. It was quite a walk, and suddenly the heavens opened, and we had to shelter from the deluge. Eventually, it eased, and we half ran the rest of the way, a bit wet when we arrived, but they had spare beds, so we checked in. I was quite shocked at the price, $35 for a cot in a cramped room, stuffed full of bunks and backpacks, smelling like a musty back alley laundrette. It was getting on, so I showered, no beer for sale and none allowed on the premises! A few of us went out for pizza, and ended up in some seedy bars, frequented by older working ladies; the phrase mutton dressed as lamb came to mind. We bought them drinks, and they were a good laugh, and we ended up having a session, before returning to crash.

Apparently, we made far too much noise last night, I was getting dirty looks from the other guests. As I was starting to prepare the free breakfast, cheap bread again, and some God awful spread, but jam was available, the manageress came, and told us we had to leave. Blimey, what is happening to hostels? We took the piss a bit, which didn't go down well, I think everybody there had had a sense of humour lobotomy? I said goodbyes to Dennis, and the others who had been with us last night, got my stuff, and went back to Penn. Might as well pay an extra $15 for a private room out in Elizabeth. So, I returned to the motel and paid for the final three days of the six months long trip, thinking that I would have been better off actually paying more for the flight, and spending less time here. Oh well, nothing to be done about it now.

Breakfast back at Sam's diner, before returning to Penn. I bought an all day subway pass and rode the train to The Bronx. I was a bit nervous going out onto the street with the past reputation of that infamous district, but it all looked normal, nice housing, and hardly anybody about. I walked around the block, not seeing anything untoward or aught that inspired me to spend time there, nothing really for a tourist, so I went back to town. The rest of that lovely spring day, I spent wandering around Central park which is massive. Joggers, horse and carriage rides, high rise all around the perimeter. Trees in full leaf, lots with blossom, and expanses of well kept lawn, and flower borders. I couldn't really afford to pay to go in anywhere, so I just satisfied myself with a gentle amble, breathing in the relatively fresh air, and enjoying the tranquility, picnickers gathered in groups, kids playing and laughing. A big lake, and other smaller ones, monuments dotted here and there. I saw the Natural history museum, and decided that was how I was going to spend my final day.

Its full name is The American Museum of Natural History, and the imposing building is neoclassical Romanesque, with columns adorning the main entrance façade. There are five floors if I remember correctly, open to the public, and you need more than one day to see everything, so I did my best. A fully engrossing day, as you can imagine, there is a shit load to take in. There are fossil halls, An Earth and space section, gems and mineral displays, anthropology, everything to do with nature that is known to humanity, and heaps more; in short, you will spend hours being intrigued by all the information that your brain is trying its best to absorb. If you are going to be in NY for a few days, I highly recommend spending a day or two there.

Something that has stuck firmly in my mind, was watching the human population growth counter. It takes a few minutes to see it from start to finish, and most of it is a flattish line that only begins its serious upward trajectory in the last couple of centuries; then it heads at a steeper angle, still north, from the 60s/ 70s onwards. The thing that was striking to me was the almost imperceptible blip that occurred at the end of 2004, after the mighty Indian ocean tsunami! Of course, subjectively, the loss of life was horrific, and provoked a deep sadness and empathy for the dead and the families of the deceased. But looking at it entirely objectively, the human population recovered its numbers in just a few days!!

So, a largely successful travel experience draws to a close. I have learnt an immense amount, including now being able to converse in a language other than English, a major achievement for me, as I historically struggled with foreign tongues. I've met some great and interesting people, found out how part of the Americas are environmentally, a mixed bag, but a lot of hope that preservation will prevail: done some excellent diving, seen a myriad of natural wonders, human enterprise and innovation.The trip didn't end with a bang, a quiet last night, and the journey home was largely uneventful.

I had fulfilled my aim of escaping the British winter, lived perfectly adequately on a small budget, there was still cash in my bank account, and I had fine tuned my ecological footprint. I get criticism for flying at all, but I'm not going to just sit at home and do nothing, though that's what we've all being doing recently; or kill myself for the sake of saving the planet, when very few other people bother to even acknowledge there is a problem. I don't have kids or carnivorous pets; yes, your dogs and cats collectively are an environmental nightmare. There are millions of people who take two short haul flights daily, to get to work, whereas I take two or three, sometimes four long haul flights yearly. I don't do fashion, a major polluting industry, that no one seems to want to talk about. Most things I do, I try to reflect how it will impact the natural world, and it's very easy to adjust your behavior with a little thought. It astonishes me for instance, how much toilet paper, shampoo and other products full of palm oil, gets used in some households.

I was going to write an afterword along the lines of the one in Wanderlust, but none of those ideas that I portrayed there have become popular yet. The illegal wildlife trade just started right back up as soon as the pandemic retreated during the summer of 2020; deforestation barely took a breather. Immediately after the fast food restaurants reopened for takeaway, litter blighted the road verges again. Food waste is still way too high, especially in Western countries; we don't need to stop eating meat, maybe reduce our intake a bit, but if wastage was eliminated, the environmental footprint for agriculture would be vastly decreased. Corporations seem to be getting more powerful, and small businesses are going to the wall. Our liberties are being eroded bit by bit, and if we don't take them back as soon as the threat of covid is gone, then we shall probably lose them forever. Some of the laws being introduced without parliamentary scrutiny are extremely worrying. The wealth gap between rich and poor widened further: yet again. And now, everybody, countries I mean, are bickering over who is going to get the vaccine. Humans are humans I suppose. It's pretty clear that there will be more outbreaks of serious new diseases and viruses, if the human species goes back to the old normal. In the last twenty years there have been several, sars, mers, bird flu, swine flu; covid is just the most recent and we didn't get control of it early enough. Prepare for more infectious disorders if we, humanity, are not going to change our behaviour. Anyway, thank you so much for reading this, there will be more to come if the sales of this one are an improvement on Wanderlust. Keep an open heart. Keep an open mind. And remember, you are the creator of your own destiny.